"It is only when we begin to experience our own t[...] of recognizing these qualities in others. This book [...] ical dig of the most personal kind, dedicated to bringing forth the authentic self in the workplace. A stunning accomplishment!"—*Nancy Kezlarian, Executive Director, Florence Crittenton Center*

"This book opens up one of the great perennial questions of human life in a way that is both spiritually sensitive and concretely practical—the question of the relationship between the inner search and the need for effective action in the world. The thoughtfulness and creativity of the applications offered by the authors sets this book apart."—*Jacob Needleman, author of* Money and the Meaning of Life *and* Time and the Soul

"Peppers and Briskin have written a creative guide for all who seek greater inspiration and soul in their work. This book is grounded in the principles of depth psychology and makes commonsense use of working with persona and shadow issues in the workplace as well as our personal lives. This book can truly provide a bridge between our inner lives and the work that we do in the world. It is no ordinary 'self-help' book, but a path for self-examination and reflection, bringing nuggets of wisdom from many sources."—*Suzy Spradlin, Ph.D., Clinical Psychologist, Analyst, C. J. Jung Institute of San Francisco*

"Beautifully written with intelligence and humor. The stories and applications open a remarkable window on today's work landscape. The book presents the reader with a path for personal renewal and a way to discover their own meaning and purpose in work."—*Cathy Chuplis, Director, Worldwide Communications, Levi Strauss & Co.*

"It is very hopeful to me that so many people are wondering about the meaning of their work, and how to bring themselves more fully into their work lives. This wonderful, gentle guide encourages us to delve deeply into these questions, and then supports us to make courageous choices. This book is both timely and timeless. We must never stop seeking for meaning, and we've been gifted with Cheryl and Alan's astute and loving expertise."—*Margaret J. Wheatley, author of* Leadership and the New Science *and coauthor of* A Simpler Way

"*Bringing Your Soul to Work* is written with care and in an easy and compelling prose. Peppers and Briskin are bravely willing to face what is difficult and confusing in life and work and therefore are very respectful to the reader. The book is a fine blend of spirit and practicality and if the reader has the will to do the exercises, they will find they will have given voice to their own story, which is the point of reading, anyway."—*Peter Block, author of* Stewardship, The Empowered Manager, *and* Flawless Consulting

"What does 'soul' have to do with going to work every day? Everything, when traditional notions of work are transformed from employment (what we do) to a process of self discovery (who we want to become). The authors raise profound issues and offer practical insight about successfully embarking on a life-changing journey through the experience of work. This book is a highly evocative and deeply personal 'field guide' to better understanding different, even difficult, parts of ourselves through what we do. It is a powerful dialogue that can help us realize more of our humanity by consciously reframing the role and purpose of work in our lives. The wisdom of this book makes a seminal contribution to anyone who wonders, 'There must be more to work life.'"—*Peter Boland, Ph.D., President, Boland Healthcare*

"Business leaders today confront a most pragmatic concern—the war for talent. Without authentic, soul-led, passionate commitment themselves, leaders cannot attract and keep people. Cheryl and Alan guide the reader first on the inner path to finding one's true voice and passion, and then offer wise counsel and simple but effective practices for taking soulfulness into the gritty world of inspiring people, managing roles and driving business.

"Today's institutions and our upbringing have not prepared us for this new economy. Instead, we feel fragmented, rushed, unsatisfied. Cheryl and Alan offer practical ways for unearthing the lost abilities to see deeply, to be authentic, to listen soulfully. Armed with the disciplines they outline, the reader can discover the narrow and rewarding path that balances authenticity and role, being and doing, intention and action."—*Stephanie Spong, Managing Director, Razorfish, Los Angeles*

"This book offers the most thoughtful integration of the concepts of 'soul' and 'work' that I have ever read. Using realistic examples with which everyone can identify, the authors demonstrate how we can learn from and transcend personal disappointments and crises related to work. Step by step, they help us recognize our self-made stumbling blocks (shadow) that prevent us from feeling good about how we relate to our jobs and the people with whom we work. By following the authors' thoughtful progression of questions and explanations, we unearth and clarify our self-defeating thoughts and behaviors, take ownership for our misguided beliefs, and discover the soul in our work lives."—*Andrea Markowitz, Ph.D., Assistant Professor of Industrial/ Organizational Psychology, University of Baltimore*

"This is a lovely book; it enables the subtle wisdom of the inner world to acknowledge and awaken the hidden, latent wisdom of the world of work. Anyone would benefit from this lyrical yet penetrating analytic exposé. It demonstrates the falsity of a dualism which separates mind from heart, or interiority from the world. It also has the generosity to invite and leave room for the reader to interact with its claims."
—*John O'Donohue, author of* Anam Cara: A Book of Celtic Wisdom *and* Eternal Echoes: Exploring Our Yearning to Belong

BRINGING
Your SOUL
TO WORK

BRINGING
Your SOUL
TO WORK

An Everyday Practice

Cheryl Peppers
Alan Briskin

BERRETT–KOEHLER PUBLISHERS, INC.
San Francisco

Berrett-Koehler Publishers, Inc.
450 Sansome Street, Suite 1200
San Francisco, CA 94111-3320
Tel: (415) 288-0260   Fax: (415) 362-2512   www.bkconnection.com

ORDERING INFORMATION

Quantity sales. Special discounts are available on quantity purchases by corporations, associations, and others. For details, contact the "Special Sales Department" at the Berrett-Koehler address above.

Individual sales. Berrett-Koehler publications are available through most bookstores. They can also be ordered direct from Berrett-Koehler: Tel: (800) 929-2929; Fax: (802) 864-7626; www.bkconnection.com

Orders for college textbook/course adoption use. Please contact Berrett-Koehler: Tel: (800) 929-2929; Fax: (802) 864-7626.

Orders by U.S. trade bookstores and wholesalers. Please contact Publishers Group West, 1700 Fourth Street, Berkeley, CA 94710. Tel: (510) 528-1444; Fax (510) 528-3444.

Printed in the United States of America

Printed on acid-free and recycled paper that is composed of 50% recovered fiber, including 10% postconsumer waste.

Library of Congress Cataloging-in-Publication Data
Peppers, Cheryl, 1959–
   Bringing your soul to work : an everyday practice / Cheryl Peppers and Alan Briskin.—1st ed.
      p. cm.
   Includes bibliographical references and index.
   ISBN 1-57675-111-2 (alk. paper)
   1. Work—religious aspects.   I. Briskin, Alan, 1954–   II. Title.
BL65.W67.B75 2000
291.4—dc21   00-033688

Book design and composition by Beverly Butterfield, Girl of the West Productions.

FIRST EDITION

05 04   03   02   01   00   10   9   8   7   6   5   4   3   2   1

For
Rebecca Briskin
and
Dr. Robert W. Gray

CONTENTS

PREFACE

T HIS BOOK began as a small project that turned into its own journey. Berrett-Koehler had asked Alan to prepare a study guide for the soft-cover publication of his first book, *The Stirring of Soul in the Workplace*. At about the same time, Cheryl was rethinking her consulting practice, looking for ways to bring understanding and renewal to those struggling for more meaning in their work. A colleague of Cheryl's turned out to be a friend of Alan's and suggested they meet. Soon, we had agreed to write a study guide together as a first step toward collaboration.

Some months into the project, we realized that we had stumbled onto something much bigger—a guide that would take readers along a personal journey, linking ideas about spirit and soul to the gritty realities of the workplace. What has gotten lost? How do we get work done amidst the demands and tugs on our soul? How do we awaken to our gifts? How do we join with others to make work meaningful? Through stories, reflections, and written applications, the guide would invite readers to take up these questions and apply them to their specific work settings. Knowing that so many are searching for ways to bring soul into their work, our goal became to provide encouragement as well as a pathway for the journey.

To listen to the soul's voice is to be mindful of our own particular path and curious about the patterns that thread our lives together. How do we follow the threads that lead into our own personal story? How can we find the place where the inner world and the outer world meet—find soul, that is, in the points of overlap? As writers, we invite readers to draw on their imagination, their curiosity, their courage, and their belief that "there must be something more."

ACKNOWLEDGMENTS

A BOOK IS an act of imagination, ideas forming into words on a page. And it is also an invisible community of friends and colleagues who give comfort and support. This book took form out of the many stories, shared experiences, and courageous acts of our clients and friends. We want to thank those of you we have had the privilege to work with, for you have often been our teachers and guides into the inner terrain of work. And we want to particularly express our appreciation for those who read early drafts and offered us guidance and new insights. These include Yvonne Allara, David Bradford, Cathy Chuplis, John Durrett, Sheryl Erickson, Jodi Farrar, Robert Farrar, Susan Harris, Marty Kaplan, Nancy Kezlarian, Mario Leal, Steve Maybury, Susan Pattee, Glenn Tobe, and Peg Umanzio.

We want to thank our agent and editorial consultant, Sheryl Fullerton, who read each chapter in its first form and guided us to deepening and clarifying the material, and also Valerie Barth, our editor at Berrett-Koehler, for her consistent support in shepherding this book from imagination to print. We also want to thank the staff at Berrett-Koehler for their creative ideas and collaborative support.

Thank you to our network of family, friends, and colleagues who offered us inspiration, conversation, and practical help. These include John Brett, Carol Briskin, Jules Briskin, Chris Cahill, Lisa and Rufus Cole, Arthur Colman, Colin Crabb, JoAnn Culbert-Koehn, Rich Dodson, Kevin Doering, Carolyn Firmin, Rachel Flaith, Carol Frenier, Jodi Gold, Myrna Holden, Amy Honigman, Michael Jones, Barbara Kaplan, Myrna Kranz, Liza Leeds, George McCauley, Chris Morgan, Kelly Morgan, Lilly Myer, Mern O'Brien, Don Peppers, Ralph Reed, Kate Regan, Gary Sattler, Stephen Schultz, Saul Siegel, Stephanie Spong, Suzy Spradlin, Mika Yoshino, and Arnold Zippel.

Alan wants to thank his wife, Jane, and his son, Alex, for their love, insight, and support through times that pulled him in many directions.

To all of you who have aided us with your gifts and encircled us with your support, we stand in appreciation for our good fortune.

INTRODUCTION

The Collective Cry for Something More

THIS BOOK ADDRESSES what many feel but cannot say out loud, that amidst the frenetic pace and constant urgencies at work, one is often left feeling barren inside. How is it that so much activity can still leave one empty? How can one live more straight from the soul without being made an outcast? And how do we go beyond simply balancing work and personal life to an approach to living that has integrity and beauty? This book suggests a way to engage an inner dialogue about self and work that is grounded in our own experience. We learn not only of an inner wilderness that has pattern and meaning, but also that we are joined with others, and it is through relationship that our souls are shaped and weathered.

Bringing Your Soul to Work: An Everyday Practice links ideas about soul to the realities of the workplace. How do we connect what is true and natural within ourselves to the demands and sacrifices required of us? How do we face the polarities, tensions, and contradictions in our work and work settings without succumbing to fragmentation or cynicism? How can we join with others to face the challenges that lie ahead? And how can we move from fear to faith? These questions haunt the collective imagination, for they are no longer about individuals alone. We face the new millennium with the twentieth century at our back, with all its contradictions and uncertainties whispering in our ear, "What now?"

Sometimes it is possible to see how contradictions and uncertainties link us to more meaning, not less. And it is sometimes by engaging these gritty realities that we discover the links between our inward, spiritual lives and the world that is outside. Consider these two divergent images. The first is from the cover of *Newsweek* nearly shouting in bold print, "WORK IS HELL." Staring out from the cover is Dilbert, with two vacant white circles for eyes, and a cartoon bubble with the word "Help." Dogbert, the cheerful and ruthless management consultant, lurks in the corner. At the turn of the millennium, the Dilbert cartoons reflect back to us images of work as an exercise in absurdity, pointlessness, and cynicism.

The second image is from a traditional business journal, *Across the Board*. We see the black silhouette of a man walking away from us, carrying a briefcase that is partly a blur. The headline reads, "Soul Searching: Looking for Meaning in the Workplace." The editor's column leaves no doubt about the changes he sees happening in the workplace. Where once employees looked to "the company" for a lifetime career, they now no longer expect job security. Where once employees may have looked for meaning outside work, they now seek it within the workplace. And where once employees looked primarily for promotion and pay increases, now it is about something more elusive and central, the search for soul: that work should resonate with a person's being.

These two images capture a social disquiet and restlessness that has stirred the workplace and beyond. Something does not seem right. Are we to be cogs in the machinery, subject to moronic bosses and techniques of manipulation? Or are we perched at the precipice of a new awareness, where caring, meaning, and stewardship actually matter? How does one dare yearn for something more, when so many workplaces seem aligned solely with financial survival and profit making? Why is it that the soul now matters? What no longer seems right?

Against these tensions, there is a popular movement gaining momentum, to bring spirituality into the workplace. The inclination for community, the need for recognition, and the longing to glimpse how life is interconnected—these forces continue to pull on us. Yet many of the approaches to spirit at work feel prescriptive, shallow, or generic. Thus despite the many books available, readers are often left to themselves to figure out what to do differently.

Bringing Your Soul to Work: An Everyday Practice encourages readers to examine the particular circumstances of their work lives and to construct meaning from their own experience. Organized around stories, reflective questions, and specific applications, it grounds readers in both imagination and practice. In this way, the book serves as a guide for bringing one's spiritual values to bear on the dilemmas of work life and for creating something new and lasting.

Bringing Your Soul to Work: An Everyday Practice is for those looking to increase their effectiveness at work and bring more feeling, imagination, and heart into their efforts with others. It is for managers who find themselves caught in the midst of turbulence, for leaders and consultants looking for new ways to foster personal and organizational renewal, and for anyone who has done significant personal reflection and is looking for more specific application to work settings. For those who have read *The Stirring of Soul in the Workplace* and other books that touch on matters of spirituality, leadership, relationship, and improving work settings, the book serves as an extension of these ideas into a personal practice. For those unfamiliar but intrigued with the subject of spirituality at work, the book offers a place to begin their exploration. Finally, it is for those wishing to dialogue about movement forward, toward a next generation of workplaces.

As authors, we have tried to be as free of jargon as possible and to present sometimes abstract, even mystical ideas in as straightforward a manner as possible. We join with readers, sharing our own personal experience in an occasional story by Alan or Cheryl.

How the Book Is Organized

Bringing Your Soul to Work: An Everyday Practice bridges the interior world of the individual with the uncertainties and demands of work. Early on, this means gaining increasing comfort with varieties of introspective activities, then using these skills to consider questions of purpose and effectiveness. As we gain comfort with our own inner wildness, the greater our capacity is to navigate the wilderness of work. The journey is meant to be transformative, offering new ways to look inward and outward, and to see more clearly how we are joined with others.

In the first chapter, we explore the mystery of soul and its historical association with the vitality of life and inward complexity, and we introduce a major premise of our book—that there are many selves, many voices within each of us, and that awareness of how they conflict and harmonize can lead to wholeness. This brings us to the book's first section, "Mapping the Territory," highlighting our interior life as a means for effectively navigating the world of work.

In "Mapping the Territory," chapter 2 shows how our capacities to think metaphorically, reflect on our experience, and use our innate imagination can lead to greater understanding in the workplace. Chapter 3 explores how we can move into a more powerful way of being by identifying the many discrete voices within us and drawing on them for specific situations. In chapters 4 through 6, we take the reader on a foray into the darker, less understood aspects of one's own personality and their implications for the work setting. We're seeking to understand what parts of ourselves we hide or reject as well as what treasures are waiting to be uncovered. In considering *shadow* as part of the whole person, we reconsider how we have judged ourselves and others. Honoring both fear and compassion in this dynamic, we invite the reader to consider alternatives to hiding from their shadow.

If we can appreciate the vastness and richness of our interior world, we are better prepared to deal with the complexity of workplace issues. In this way, the first section serves as a foundation for the second, "The Expedition."

In "The Expedition," chapter 7 bridges what matters within to what brings us satisfaction and purpose at work. Purpose allows for renewal, bringing us the energy to shape and reshape what we do. In chapter 8, we explore how to step into a new work role and pay attention to both our own internal signals and those from the organization. Chapter 9 presents practices for being focused and effective in our role. Chapter 10 captures the dynamic energy of group life and how the difficulties and rewards of being in groups forges who we are. In our final chapter, we suggest that these reflections and practices open up our hearts and allow us to shape and endure, with grace, the continuum of experience we encounter in work and life.

Using This Book

Bringing Your Soul to Work: An Everyday Practice is written with pauses for reflection and specific application. Some readers will wish to journal their reflections and work in depth, while others will read the reflections or applications and move on to the next sections. We assume that each person will determine their own best rhythm for working with the material. Both the stories and the questions for reflection have a way of staying in one's mind and popping up at unusual times. Implicit to our writing is the assumption that the reader will slow down and use the material for reflection. To aid this, we suggest the following:

1. For some of the reflections and applications, it's important to be in a quiet setting, free of distractions—perhaps somewhere in your home that feels comfortable or where you normally read or meditate, or perhaps in an office with the door closed and the

telephone ringer turned off. For other reflections, an airplane commute might be fine.

2. If a question doesn't seem clear or relevant to you, or if you feel stuck for very long on how to answer it from your own experience, simply move on. You may find its relevance later. Likewise, if an application seems confusing or frustrating, others may flow more easily for you.

3. Keeping a journal will aid your learning. Throughout the book, you will find questions for deeper reflection marked with a magnifying glass—☀—and applications that are best written out marked with a journal page—☐. When doing the applications especially, writing your responses should help you to anchor into your own experience more concretely, as well as to retain certain concepts. For some people, however, writing is not an effective mode for absorbing material. If you choose not to write your responses, try to take time for adequate reflection.

4. If you find yourself wanting to hurry through the reflections and applications, it might be worthwhile to consider the reasons. Some of the richest insights emerge while patiently sifting through difficult material. Is your wanting to hurry simply because you've done a lot of reflection in your life already? Do you feel impatient or judgmental? Is there something you'd rather avoid? (The answer to this last question is always "yes," by the way.)

5. It's important, when doing the applications, to be open and somewhat playful or imaginative in your approach. Many of the questions are directed at a way of knowing that is different from rational, analytical thinking. Using the emotional and intuitive requires a certain spirit of playfulness and a nonjudgmental attitude.

6. When reading something that especially strikes you but you're not sure why, take time to pause and reflect on what might be going on in your life that is being touched upon.

7. Finally, try to remember that the nature of discovery is an unfolding process, not necessarily called up on demand. Be

gentle with yourself, patient with your answers, alert for insights that might emerge later, and expectant that your understanding will deepen over time and with practice.

1

The Inner
Wilderness
of Soul

The journey is difficult, immense, at times impossible,
yet that will not deter some of us from attempting it. . . .
I can at best report only from my own wilderness.
The important thing is that each man possess such
a wilderness and that he consider what marvels are
to be observed there.[1]

—LOREN EISELEY

OUR LIVES ARE MARKED with a series of events, encounters, and turning points that in one way or another stamp our outlook on life and move us in this direction or that. Ultimately, our responses to those events shape us into who we are today. If we can view these circumstances of our lives as aspects of our very own story, our unique pathway through life, then we can make the journey more conscious, and we can open to it. As Loren Eiseley has suggested, the only vantage point for the journey is "from my own wilderness." If we imagine our own inner wilderness as a base camp, this book is about the exploration of that personal wilderness and going out into the wilderness of our work lives. It's about beholding the wonders and dangers, bringing the journey into consciousness. Perhaps we shall also discover something about soul!

If you are unsure of what this word *soul* means and yet find yourself strangely drawn to it—especially with regard to using it in the same sentence as *workplace*—you are not alone. There are about as many meanings for the word *soul* as there are people taking up the question. Rather than that being a deterrent, it actually serves a useful purpose: Without the complications of a technical, rational understanding, the word *soul* can be a metaphor that feeds directly into our longings for meaning and purpose. In this way, it serves as something of a projection screen from which we can each envision our own particular meaning.

 Reflection

GETTING STARTED

- WHAT MEANING does soul have for you? How would you describe it?
- WHAT IS currently stirring in your life that draws your attention to a book such as this?

How We Describe Soul

There is a lot of talk these days about soul and spirit, with many different concepts thrown around rather loosely. Teasing out some of the historical meanings behind the words can help us get grounded for the journey ahead. The meaning and context of the words themselves have crossed over into each other in different ways, at different times, and in different cultures. Our interest is not so much in distinguishing the use of one word from another historically as it is to clarify how we are using the word soul in this book. Accordingly, the following table highlights distinguishable themes for how the word soul has been

Historical Themes of Soul

Theme	Origins	Examples
The underworld, depth, shadowy realities; connection to unconscious facets of ourselves	Early Greek	Homer's *Odyssey*, the necessity of journey into Hades. Carl Jung wrote, "The dread and resistance which every natural human being experiences, when it comes to delving too deeply into himself is, at bottom, the fear of the journey to Hades."[2] Soul as metaphor for our own personal odyssey, the journey into the darkness of our own underworld.
Vitality, source of animation, essence, renewal, transmutation, and metamorphosis	Greek, Hindu, and American Indian stories	Latin root *anima* (animation) meant *breath* or *soul*. Greek word for *soul*, *psyche*, also meant *butterfly*, indicating its gentle nature, ability to take flight, capacity for metamorphosis. Soul as metaphor for what happens if we *don't* attend to our authentic selves: the deeper parts of our soul no longer animate us; the soul takes flight.
Union of opposites, joining spirit and matter, light and dark aspects of the whole person; the rhythm and driving power in nature	Hebrew, African, Buddhist, and Taoist philosophy	Hebrew words *adamah*, "dust of the ground"; *ruach*, "breath of life" and "spirit"; and *nephesh*, "living soul"; suggestion of living soul created by breathing divinity/spirit into what is fashioned out of the muck of the earth. Hebrew creation story implies the coming together of divinity and humanity, spirit and body. Soul as metaphor for coping with the contradictions and limitations of modern life; holding together the middle between the material and spiritual. Soul as a path to awakening and higher consciousness. Soul as an earthly form of divinity and the rhythm of life.
Spark of the divine, qualities of supreme being, cosmic aspect to consciousness	Gnostic myths, indigenous traditions, Hindu and Christian beliefs	Creation story of light fragments hurtling through the universe and lodging as divine sparks within our souls. Transcendence; mystery of rebirth; reincarnation; patterns of the eternal; knowing beyond the physical. Philosophical source for questions of origin and destiny, the meaning of life. Soul as metaphor for being connected with something larger; a reminder that our lives are not our own.

used in the past, suggesting how, in this book, we might draw upon these meanings.

Notable themes of soul relevant to our work here include the journey into the shadowy nature of our inner world, vitality and renewal, the union of opposites, and elements of transcendence. Though they span several thousand years, these themes remain current. In a time of emphasis upon external impressions, it is appropriate to go inward; in a time of lost authenticity at work, to seek renewal; in a time of linear, absolute thinking, to consider the relationship of opposites; and in a time of constrictions from all of the above, to open to the transcendent.

A popular response to the increasing turbulence at work is to turn to spiritual answers. Though attending to the spiritual has value, it can also have limitations. It may be used to avoid the tough issues at work, or become a new form of rhetoric, or be confused with religious observance, or even pit groups against each other. Sometimes, it seems, a common thread in the popular movement is to take the focus away from actual work—to take time out for poetry, for walks in nature, for opening to the heart's calling regarding "real work," or for praying or meditating with others at work. When the subject is more directly related to work itself, it frequently manifests in the form of achieving one's highest potential, attaining power and wealth, managing stress, and even developing "emotional intelligence." One gets the feeling that to be spiritual at work requires either being away from work entirely (ironic) or doing a significant amount of additional work (equally ironic). The question remains, dangling for us to figure out for ourselves, of how to bridge the painful distance between our spiritual lives and our work lives.

There is a valid place for a spirituality that emphasizes time apart from the ordinary routines of work, including time for rest, reflection, rejuvenation. Certainly the idea of a "Sabbath rest" makes intuitive sense. In the face of today's work demands, a case could be made for spirituality as a complete flight from work and not merely as a Sabbath rest. Such a stance reflects the seeming impossibility of actually bridging the two worlds; we are left instead with having to choose between them. Unfortunately, this dilemma is all too real for many people today, quite possibly for you personally. Yet it is here, in this dilemma, that we are most vulnerable to a form of spirituality that is a disservice—when focus on the spiritual leads to a flight away from the more difficult realities requiring our attention. How does one embrace the spiritual without simply fleeing from the challenges and difficulties that mark our lives?

Spirit can suggest our highest potential, a place described by the Dalai Lama as a land of high, white peaks. But spirit needs to be joined with the fertile fields and hidden valleys of our own experience. Soul, as a concept distinct from spirit, draws on imagination, passion and reflection to remind us that life is a constant tension among opposite pulls. To approach the soul means to go deeper, on an odyssey of self-discovery that connects us to the world and our duties in life. Soul introduces us to mystery, it leads us to our own darkness, and it reveals new possibilities. In soul, we find the threads that weave together those fundamental questions of life: Where have I been? Where am I going? What truly matters? What do I want?

Soul beckons us straight into the swampy muck where our inner life and our work life intersect. This space is often marked with uncertainty and is sometimes dark, absent of the light clarity brings. Yet soul is the space in which the most fertile materials are found, the space which offers the possibility for renewal and vitality. It is in delving directly into the gritty realities of contradiction and uncertainty at work that one is able to bring spirituality into work life. The swamp is a provocative metaphor. Henry David Thoreau wrote, "When I would recreate myself, I seek the darkest wood, the thickest and most interminable, and to the citizen, most dismal swamp. I enter the swamp as a sacred place—a *sanctum sanctorum*. There is the strength, the marrow of nature."[3]

Learning to hold the material and spiritual worlds together in creative tension is an act of courage and a form of love. Embedded in the idea of soul, therefore, is the sacredness of connecting the complexity of our own inner world with the complexity of the outer world. We grapple at the boundary, the overlap between self and other, the permeable line between what is inside and what is out there in the world. This can be especially difficult in the context of modern work life, with the polarization that has developed between the material and the spiritual, and with the constant shifting of boundaries around our work groups. To approach soul in organizational life is to become mindful of the web of relationships, beginning within and connecting into larger and larger circles of participation.

THE MYSTERY OF OUR MANY SELVES

When we speak of "myself" or "me" or "I," we usually assume a singular voice. Yet it may be worth considering that there are many voices, many selves, inside each of us. The question "Who am I?" is a surface question that masks a deep and interior territory. Poet and philosopher John O'Donohue wrote: "It is one of the unnoticed achievements of daily life to keep the wild complexity of your real identity so well hidden that most people never suspect the worlds that collide in your heart."[4] In literature, Virginia Woolf opened up new literary vistas by introducing to readers the wonder and beauty of characters revealed by their stream of consciousness and capacity for interior dialogue. And in the field of psychology, Carl Jung sought to demonstratethat we achieve wholeness through a personal relationship that develops among the different voices inside ourselves. Indeed, creativity and soul are intimately related to our capacity for this kind of introspection.

When there becomes too great a discrepancy between the life we lead and the worlds that collide in our heart, we can experience life and work as flat and superficial. The pull to conform to a singular self and fit in are powerful forces within the work world. Yet if we silence the varied voices within, can we really wonder why we feel empty? The greater we will ourselves to conform to an outer world, the greater the void grows within.

If we imagine our interior selves as a community of voices, how would they sound? Would we hear an uncomfortable silence, voices fed up and disrespectful of each other or alive with debate and dialogue? The invitation to attend to and learn about our many selves certainly carries a caution—fragmentation, internal civil war, an inability to please everyone. Yet beyond the battles lie the awe and satisfaction in discovering our own interior mystery.

Reflection
CHECKING OUR PULSE

- IS THERE a part of you that wants to take a kind of Sabbath rest from the issues in the workplace? Why?

- IS THERE a part of you that wants to flee entirely from a focus on work and turn your attention toward spiritual development or other matters?

- IS THERE a part of you that is willing to go into the muck, that fertile and creative space that can also be uncomfortable?

The Journey Ahead

This book is about the journey inward and the search for outward, meaningful connection in our work. Inevitably what we find affects us, so that the journey shifts, changes focus, beckons us to new directions. It is not linear. Though surprises can be frightening as well as enlightening, they are often the channels through which we catch glimpses of our deepest wilderness. The challenges of the workplace today provide many opportunities for making the journey real in our lives.

The journey is about ownership—of our inner world and the ways in which our inner world links outward. In those links, the spiritual and material coexist: Ownership makes possible the coming together of our spiritual lives and our work lives.

In the next chapters of this book, we will be gathering tools for the journey—initiating ourselves into the practice of seeing in new ways and exploring the many aspects of our multiplicity of selves. We do this by learning to approach the soul indirectly, while cultivating the skill of inward awareness. And we do it with an eye toward work—both how we understand ourselves in the context of work challenges and how we might bring more of our inner richness to bear on them.

> *There is not as much wilderness*
> *out there as I wish there were.*
> *There is more inside*
> *than you think.*[5]
>
> —DAVID BROWER

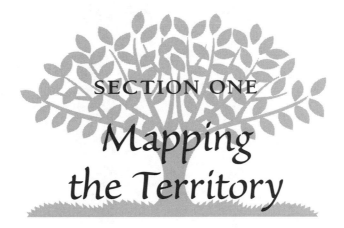

SECTION ONE

Mapping the Territory

2

Windows
to the Soul

No one really knows what the soul is,
but tremble forth it does and, just as
mysteriously, shudders away again.[1]

—PHIL COUSINEAU

How does one approach the soul? Located in that transitional space between matter and spirit, between a concrete experience and its deeper meaning, soul can hardly be approached directly. Nor can we grasp soul in its entirety. Even if we could, the nature of soul is fluid, taking new form as our experiences change and our insights deepen. How, then, shall we attempt this journey into the soul, and how can we begin to understand soul in our work experience?

In this chapter, we explore techniques for peering into the soul indirectly, each technique offering a unique vantage point. It is much like peering through the windows of a house into its various rooms.

Each picture contributes toward an image of the whole interior of the house, but the person looking in knows that there are still areas not seen—the basement, the bathrooms, the closets, perhaps an inner library. The entirety of the house remains a mystery, yet one is able to have a fairly realistic perspective by stepping up to the house one window at a time.

But soul is more than just an inner world. It is a realm in which the interior of the individual and the outer world overlap. In this sense, we can think of the house as a metaphor for the soul, a place where we live in both a private and an interactive sense.

This chapter introduces three of the many "windows" to the soul—the windows of our experience, of metaphor, and of fantasy. In each section, we will examine ways to take up the journey in the context of our work lives.

The Window of Our Experience

Mark was excited to join a large, prestigious consulting firm at the senior manager level, with the understanding that in two years he would be eligible for partnership. The partner who "found" him and hired him, Robert, had promised to personally groom him by making sure he got into the visible projects and high-level client meetings. Confident, smart, and energetic, Mark saw himself as having an opportunity to prove his savvy and instinct for tough business situations.

Soon after joining the firm, Mark was given the lead on a project with major visibility. This would be just the proving ground that Mark needed. The first few weeks of the project went well, and just as Robert had promised, Mark was given free and frequent access to the senior leadership of the chemical conglomerate client.

Several weeks into the project, Mark discovered a problem in their approach to the profit viability of a planned acquisition. Mark immediately spoke about the matter with Robert, who listened with concern and agreed to set up a meeting as soon as possible with the chief operating officer. The next day, Mark asked Robert about the meeting, and Robert stalled, suggesting that they may need more time to think about it internally on the consulting team. When nothing happened, Mark asked again and began to find Robert more and more resistant about setting up the meeting. Finally, Robert admitted that he thought it best that he, Robert, meet with the COO, lead partner to lead client, and that they had in fact arranged to have dinner that evening. Mark was not invited.

Disappointed but recognizing the sensitivity of the matter and still being new to the firm, Mark decided that there was little for him to do at the moment to challenge the situation. Over time, however, Mark found that he was regularly left out of the critical meetings and that approaching Robert about it seemed to create more difficulty. Finally, Mark learned from a trusted colleague that Robert had a reputation for promising senior managers access to client leaders, but then merely using them until it was no longer convenient to his own power base.

Mark was devastated. As he struggled to make sense of the situation, he found one illusion after another dropping away, until he was left with a darker view of the firm and also of himself. He realized that he had idealized Robert as the person who would personally mentor him through an important part of his career, but instead this experience left him feeling isolated and alone. He also had idealized his image of himself, in particular being strong and in control. Rather than the tough, savvy, forward-looking business manager he had imagined himself to be, he now also saw a person vulnerable to deception and capable of being used. Shaken by this new view of himself, Mark struggled to stay focused on the work.

With time and reflection, Mark continued to discover aspects of his own personality that were previously hidden: His self-confidence, he now understood, had elements of arrogance. Where previously he had imagined being needed for his intelligence and assertiveness, he now saw this as his own need to be important. More than simply being seduced by Robert's promises, he had been seduced by his own need to be special. Even his desire to do excellent work was related to his need for approval.

Rather than dwelling on these insights as utterly damning, Mark began to see them as a missing link in his own development. It was as if he'd found the other half of himself. At first awkward and unsettling, these new insights began to offer a different kind of self-confidence, one that was more realistic, grounded, and balanced. Released from his idealizations, he was freed to express his strengths in more effective ways and to feel less vulnerable to the seductions inherent in work life. Looking back, he came to appreciate *disillusionment* as his teacher: It pointed out his idealizations, took him through a period of disorientation, and led him to a less inflated but more solid view of himself and the firm. Clearly, the initially devastating situation had become a key catalyst in Mark's professional development.

The story of Mark* is a story each of us has experienced personally, to some extent. It is the story of coming up against disappointment and a loss of confidence that shakes us deeply. The journey of the soul often begins with the experience of being lost. We see the world and ourselves in new ways and suffer through a period of disorientation as we integrate the lessons learned. The poet Mary Oliver wrote that we see the world, for the second time, the way it really is. Her words suggest the importance of reflection on experience as a means of stripping away pretense and being freed from attitudes that distort our ability to engage life as it really is. Although rarely comfortable at the time, emotions such as disappointment and insecurity act as teachers, freeing us to reorder our world, both internally and externally.

Application
REFLECTING ON OUR EXPERIENCE

The skill of working with experience includes the capacity to suspend judgment, to take up more of an observer role, and to limit simple "good-bad," "right-wrong" reactions to what we think and feel. In this three-part application, you'll have an opportunity to examine, as Mark did, the meaning of an important experience in your life.

---

* Based on real people and actual incidents, cases in this book are sometimes composites, with elements of the story changed for reasons of confidentiality.

The first glimpse through this window of reflection is an attempt to recapture the experience fully, in your memory and emotion. Think back to a time when you were presented with a challenge that troubled you and influenced the direction of your life—preferably a difficult work situation, something imposed upon you, not of your own choosing. Think back to the experience, to that initial point where you were jostled out of the comfort zone. Take a moment to remember it, to reflect on what that experience was like for you at the time, and then take your time as you move through the questions below. Writing your answers in your journal will help to make this a more concrete experience for you.

How did the challenge first present itself—or, what made you realize that this was a challenge? (*Examples: I was asked to relocate, or I had a poor performance review, or someone at work didn't want to work with me. . . .*)

What did you experience when confronted with this challenge? (*Examples: I felt angry, or I felt confused, . . . invisible, . . . inadequate.*)

Who were the key players in this challenge? For each one, what did that person actually say or do that was significant to your experience? (*Examples: Karen, a colleague, said she agreed with me but complained to John later; Bill, my boss, withheld information; Steve, a dotted-line boss, supported me publicly but blamed the implementation problems on my managerial style.*)

How did you feel about each person? Try to identify the emotions you experienced, not just your thoughts or analysis. (*Examples: I felt angry, that I'd been duped by Karen, . . . hurt, . . . betrayed. . . .*)

How did you feel about yourself, going through this challenge? Apart from how you felt about the challenge or about others involved, what emotions did you have about you? (*Examples: I felt fragile, . . . worried, . . . uncomfortable.*)

PAUSE TO take in the experience as you felt it, as this challenge was coming on. Let your mind go wherever it wants to go. Is there more that is important to remember?

Was it difficult to bring the memories back to awareness? Reflecting on what it was like to move through this application, do you detect openness, defensiveness, justification, curiosity?

The second part of this application takes us to the vantage point of how this difficult experience affected your life. Mark identified several insights that changed how he viewed himself and the world in which he worked. Moving the story forward, pause to consider the point at which you felt circumstances to be more or less resolved. Perhaps you'd settled on a new course, a new direction; something had shifted. When you're ready, consider the next set of questions.

WHAT IS the nature of the impact that this challenge had on your work and on your life? *How* was the direction of your career and/or your life influenced?

IN MEETING the challenge presented to you, what did you discover about yourself in the process?

WHAT'S DIFFERENT about *you* now, as a result of going through this challenge? Would the same circumstances be so challenging today?

WHAT FEELINGS toward yourself do you have now, in reflecting on how the challenge has influenced your development?

Examining an experience or event in terms of its meaning for us enables us to fold it into our life story. Much more valuable to us than the rude disruption that may have defined our initial experience, it becomes woven into the fabric of our journey. This final part of the application focuses on gathering the scattered pieces of our experience and folding them into our story.

Holding on to the discoveries you've identified, rewind the tape of your story back to the beginning again. Remembering both the difficulty of the experience as it happened and the consequent discoveries that influenced your life, consider the following.

IF YOU could change the course of events, would you erase the entire story? That means, of course, giving up what you have discovered about yourself and life as well as giving up the difficulties of the challenge. Would you trade them both in? Why or why not?

WHO OR what were your teachers in this story? Who or what provoked your learning? (*Example: Disillusionment was a teacher for Mark; Robert's behavior and Mark's own loss of confidence had led to his learning.*)

GIVEN YOUR answers to the two questions above, how would you summarize the meaning that this experience has had for you? That is, how does it fit into the story of your life?

WHAT ARE your feelings toward the totality of your experience, at this point?

ON RE-MEMBERING OUR EXPERIENCE

The world we live in is fragmented, and there is constant pressure upon us to "not be" a certain way, or to "not think" a certain way. As we succumb to this pressure to tone down our feelings or discount our experience, we lose pieces of who we are, and we lose our experience of ourselves. By reflecting on our experience, we are gathering back the pieces that have been cast aside, dismembered. Thus we honor our experience, re-membering who we are.

The Window of Metaphor

Metaphor enables the evocative language of soul, using images in one figure of speech to describe new and deeper ways of understanding experience. Meaning in a physical event is extended beyond just the event itself. Shakespeare wrote, "All the world's a stage, and all the men and women merely players: They all have their exits and their entrances." He captured in a physical image the notion that individual lives unfold against a larger, shared experience of human development. In this chapter, we use *window* as a metaphor for viewing something that is not out in the open for direct view but, rather, is inside, hidden in partial darkness, personal, mysterious. Metaphor and analogy allow us to see indirectly into what may be initially invisible, to leapfrog from the known to the unknown and back again—to stumble into new meanings that we might not ordinarily think about.

Cheryl's Story

A T 7:30 in the morning on New Year's Day, I looked out from my third-floor, Southern California apartment across the marina to see an old man lazily crisscrossing the channel in a small, homemade-looking sailboat. I found this to be a rather curious sight, wondering who would be doing such a thing at that hour of the morning on that particular day. Then I found myself wondering whether he'd stayed up all night and was starting off the New Year in this way with any sort of intentional significance, or whether he just had nothing better to do and couldn't sleep. I started wondering about his life, whether he'd built the boat, what he was thinking about. . . . Finally, my awareness turned to how intrigued—even moved—I was by this real-life image. There must be something here for me, I thought.

At that point, I opened to the question of what this image might be saying to me, at a deeper level, as a metaphor of my own life experience. There was something important for me about how this man seemed to enjoy the simplicity of life in the moment—a bathtub-sized boat with a sail resembling an old sheet, a small breeze, a quiet morning—and about how he took his time crossing back and forth across the channel. It reminded me of the zigzag nature of my career. My first thought was critical of myself, that I ought to have laid out a straighter career path. But as I took in this image, I saw that sometimes the best route is back and forth. This was an important insight, for I was right in the middle of a major transition in my career. It reminded me to take time to enjoy the simple pleasures of life, to take in the stillness, to "build my life" with the tools and materials I have, and to be grateful for the course through life that I have taken. Though not straight, it has provided the experiences that have prepared me for my work today. ✤

We learn through metaphor that we can shift our attention back and forth at any given time between the concrete and the imaginative. Our willingness to shift enables us to let go of the views that have restrained us and to open to new ways of seeing, reflecting, and understanding.

There are two levels of reflection that we can practice when working with metaphor: The first level is to practice creating the metaphors themselves, in which we associate what we see concretely with new meanings. The second level is to reflect on what is happening emotionally within us that led us to create certain metaphors and not others. Contact with nature, as poets can attest, can be a powerful point of entry for those learning to draw understanding from metaphor.

Alan's Story

WHEN WALKING on the beach, I often cannot help but think about what I see in terms of what I'm experiencing in my life. If I'm in a mode of deep thought, I might consider the unfathomable nature of the ocean, its depths, the vastness of what is unknown, the richness of its mystery and life—and I feel awe and wonder. Or if I'm feeling uneasy, I might experience what I see as a metaphor for the struggle to survive—pelicans diving into the water, needing to fill their bellies; fish (imagined) either trying to avoid being eaten or looking for other fish to eat. Alternatively, I also might see the diving birds as seeking nourishment from what lies below the surface. My moods often reflect themselves in the metaphors I imagine and, conversely, my metaphors can often affect my moods. Either way, reflecting on what I see in nature allows me to see into myself in new ways. ❧

Reflection
NATURE AS METAPHOR

Consider taking a walk to one of your favorite spots outdoors. Pay attention to your thoughts and feelings just before the experience in nature, as well as whether you were alone or with others, what was happening—anything that may influence your experience going in. While on your nature visit, take in what you see, what you hear, smell, taste, touch. Open yourself to make comparisons—"The birds remind me of . . ." or "The trash . . ." or whatever it is that you see. Then, take some time to ponder the experience afterward, giving yourself permission to "play" with the images. (If it's not possible to create an experience in nature at this time, you might reflect on a previous experience and recall some of the sights and sounds, as well as what was going on around you before the experience.)

- WHAT DID you see, physically?
- WHAT DID you hear?
- WHAT SMELLS or sensations do you remember, perhaps the feeling of touch (with wind or water, for example)?
- WHAT DO you think this experience may have been saying to you? What metaphors arise naturally?

If a metaphor about your work life didn't come up for you spontaneously, consider what work-related metaphor might be available in your experience of nature.

You've just gazed into your soul through the window of metaphor. In public speaking, metaphors are a powerful way of communicating concepts, because they provide the audience with a more concrete, visual way to experience and remember the points. In *soul work,* the experience is less concrete, our inner complexity shifting in and out of focus. Nevertheless, an image that comes to mind at just the right time can be comforting, providing a way for us to understand our experience. In this way, an image functions as a kind of container, to hold the experience and make it easier for us to examine it.

Consider that any moment can be an opportunity for seeing through metaphor. After finishing this paragraph, look around to observe your surroundings. Are there other people around? Animals? Activity? Are you in an office—a small one, confined, or an office with windows? Or are you at home, resting in cozy furniture? Applying the same concepts as in the last reflection, consider: What do you see? What do you hear? Smell, taste, touch? Be open to making comparisons about your life. What strikes you? What do you see that is beyond the visible? What metaphors in this setting speak to you about your work life?

It's helpful to take a playful approach to metaphor. In permitting silly, even strange ideas to enter our mind, we create the kind of environment that is most open and available to whatever the psyche wants to present.

Application

AN ORDINARY WORK SETTING AS METAPHOR

The work setting provides numerous opportunities for attending to ordinary experience in a deeper way, as a window into the invisible world. Consider which meeting on your calendar might serve for the purpose of seeing through metaphor—preferably a regularly scheduled meeting and one that is not too far out on your calendar. Before going into the meeting, review these suggestions.

- In the meeting, pay attention to what you see, what you hear, how it's like "this" or "that" in your life, or how it's like what you avoid in your life.

- With one eye on the experience as a metaphor, make sure the other eye is focused on your responsibilities. That is, participate as you normally would.

- Include in your observations the layout of the room, the lighting, and so on—not just people.

- Include observations about yourself and your behaviors in the metaphor—don't make it about "them."

- Try to think of the meeting as a single unit of experience, of which you are a part.

- Be careful about judging others or yourself too harshly, as well as about speaking your thoughts outright. Your new insights may not necessarily be understood or appreciated.

- Finally, having read these tips, don't try to remember them. Instead, get into a state of "being"—be open, be observant, and be yourself.

After the meeting is concluded, consider your observations. Writing your responses to the following questions might help connect your concrete observations to deeper insights.

WHAT DID you notice that you ordinarily might not have noticed?

IN THE most general way, what metaphors or analogies arose about the meeting, the room in which the meeting was held, and the interactions of people? (Examples: The meeting room was like a bread box with no air, or like a fishbowl where everything you say or do is watched, or like a jar with a lid that you'd hit if you jumped up too high by thinking differently from others.)

WHAT METAPHORS or analogies were used in the meeting? (Examples: Expressions like "getting rid of the fat," "cut to the chase," or almost any image introduced as "It's like. . . .") What meaning do you attribute to how they were used? (To inspire? To conceal?)

WHAT OTHER images and meanings come to mind from this experience?

HOW MIGHT these metaphors and perceptions speak to you about yourself? (*Are the things you notice indicative of your feelings about being with these people? Were you glad to be there? Did you feel questioned or ignored or rejected? What in your observations might be indicative of your role or your work?*)

BE MINDFUL OF THE USE AND IMPLICATIONS OF METAPHORS

Often we take the use of metaphors for granted. As an example, "getting rid of the fat" may be stated as a need but also may neglect the value that fat brings. In trimming the fat, is something of the flavor lost? In trimming people, what do we lose in the texture and flavor of the organization? And finally, what is the meaning in comparing people to fat?

The ability to stay with our own experience, rather than dismiss it, devalue it, or leave it, allows us to tap into a richer experience—to render visible what was previously invisible. Using metaphor in an ordinary, frustrating experience can be extremely useful in this context, helping us to shift from judgment to observation.

Alan's Story

AFTER SPEAKING at a conference on business and spirituality, I decided to attend a session on the visionary leader. The speaker went on about the importance of going into work fully energized, positive, radiating with spiritual vigor, that "people want that kind of a leader!" Annoyed and filled up with judgment about the shallowness of this "cheerleader" approach, I was tempted to walk out. Uncomfortable, but reluctant to leave, I began to explore the metaphor of a cheerleader and consider how it might inform me about what was going on. "If this guy is a cheerleader," I wondered, "how is he doing? Are people cheered? Do they want this, like this?" Looking around, I saw that most people had their eyes glued on him. They responded to him, laughing or smiling or frowning at the appropriate cues. "What is it exactly," I pondered, "that is stirred in people? What is the need that is tapped into with this kind of motivational talk?" And attending to my own personal experience, I asked myself, "What part of me wants to criticize this? What part of me feels competitive? What part of me wants to be like this, to cheer people on and be cheered by their response?" I still found the situation uncomfortable. But in shifting my vantage point, I became aware of the buttons in me that had been pushed. I found I could also identify with the speaker. It was sobering but also liberating, seeing that what I had judged contained something I also envied. ❧

There is nothing so rich for glimpsing the inner wilderness of soul as ordinary experience, if we can learn to see beyond the visible. We can all learn to appreciate this simple lesson—how metaphor reflects back images of our life in more profound ways. Whether a crisscrossing sailboat or an annoying speaker, a stifling meeting or an initiative to trim the fat, we learn through metaphor to see beyond the obvious. And once alert to metaphors and their power, we begin to notice them more and can draw on them to help us navigate our journey in work life.

The Window of Fantasy

Though there are multiple paths to the soul, none are completely rational or direct. Of the three windows presented in this chapter, fantasy may seem the least rational: Fantasy encourages us to play freely with images, much like the possibilities that are available to cartoon characters. Anything can happen in a cartoon. In free-association fantasy, we open to *anything* that comes to mind in association with something else—which, as it usually turns out, is the *anything* that our unconscious wants to uncover for the benefit of our learning. Fantasy can also mean consciously considering the absurd or whatever would seem to represent the opposite of rationality or rhetoric. The story below is an example of drawing on the absurd, as well as of the playful spirit that is helpful when working with fantasy.

Alan's Story

*O*N THE final day of a conference I attended on empowerment, we were instructed to put on a skit satirizing typical change management strategies. The tone and atmosphere of the conference had been quite serious, so I was surprised and felt challenged by the request. I quickly partnered with a manager from an entertainment company, and we created a mock inspirational event, complete with an 800 number called 1-800-Mission, in which anyone could find a personal or organizational mission tailored to their own unique needs. We promised cubicles with potted plants, stereos playing stirring sound tracks, and a choice of *Rocky* posters. I exhorted the group to realize that the future was ahead of us and that establishing our sincerity was the cornerstone to being able to sell products we didn't believe in. As people watched, the earnest and serious conference mood gave way to uncontrolled laughter, hand clapping, and raucous shouts. The fantasy event was received so enthusiastically, we had to wonder afterward what deeper layer of emotion we had tapped into. It seems that some truths can only be witnessed through exaggeration, and the use of fantasy had given us permission to tap into fears and longings that were not being expressed. ❧

In this story, the atmosphere had been quite serious when the conference leader invited others to attend to the fantasy level of the work. Satirizing "typical strategies" was a way of waking up the unexpressed thoughts and feelings in the group. Attendees were willing to share the ridiculous notions that popped into their heads—and the result? Gales of laughter broke out and the energy in the conference shifted, allowing for deeper connection and more sincere dialogue among the participants.

Fantasy is not always so downright funny, of course. It can elicit any type of emotion. The point here is that fantasy requires a willingness to set aside rational understanding—to *play*, to indulge an image without judgment, for the purpose of seeing what unfolds. Playfulness is especially important for this next application, in viewing soul through the window of fantasy.

Application
PERCEPTIONS OF SOUL IN FANTASY

Open your journal and pick up a pen. Ready? Without stopping to think, begin writing a story about *anything*. It can begin with "Once upon a time," or "Joan sat on the steps outside her house," or "The killer stood lurking behind the bushes"—*anything that comes to mind is okay*. Then continue writing for three minutes. *Without* reading ahead to the next set of questions or instructions, simply make a note of the time on your watch and begin. (There is no wrong way to do this.)

*Write your three-minute story
before reading ahead.*

Before examining your three-minute story, consider the following.

- Because you had little time to think and plan, this application presented an opportunity for your unconscious to present "unknown" material for your open review—as if you had awakened with this dream. If you sat for a long time thinking before writing, this next point still holds.

- Everything in this story is about you. It is from you. It is all your material, whether you recognize it consciously or not, whether you were a character in the story or not, whether you like it or not—it doesn't matter, it's *all* you. If it weren't you, you would not have thought of it—simple as that. Dreams work the same way. To illustrate, let's just say you had written a story about terrorists invading the Ukraine, killing children and stealing nuclear warheads. Here are a few questions you might ask of yourself. *What part of you feels invaded, terrorized? What part of you feels foreign, perhaps powerful but distant or dangerous? What child-part of you might be in danger, or what might you be killing off within yourself? What part of you wants to take control, take action? What were the ultimate motives of the terrorists? Did they intend to destroy the world or to protect the warheads from others who did?* Even though you may have made up that story in a flash and you're not a character in it, there is clearly a wealth of soul material available about you through this window of fantasy—even about what it might mean that you're not a character in it. Whatever your three-minute story, therefore, you can be certain that it is *all* about you and that there are gifts waiting.

- If you are feeling some anxiety at this point, that is very normal. It usually comes from fear of the unknown—fear of meeting up with parts of ourselves that we dislike, or parts that we have not even allowed ourselves to admit *exist*. (Yet we know enough to react in fear.) Most often, we dislike or fear these parts because we do not really *know* them; with familiarity, we recognize their value. These are elements of our *shadow*, the subject of future chapters. It is our wilderness.

By definition, it is wild and unknown, therefore possibly ter-
rifying.

- Examining these parts is a kind of taming process. For now, try
  to approach any feared elements in a spirit of inquisitiveness.

- Usually we are able to understand what's been hidden only
  one piece at a time, other pieces remaining a mystery. What
  is ready to be known is often what shows up through images
  and dreams. What we are not ready for will remain hidden,
  appearing when we are ready to digest it. The psyche is
  wonderful that way, offering up a steady stream of gifts for
  integration into our consciousness, one gift at a time.

You are now ready to play the role of observer to the story
you have spontaneously created. The objectivity of the observer
role will help keep you honest about which aspects of the story
to consider. *It may not always be comfortable, but this part of our
work is crucial: The ability to take up an observer role is central to
the task of soul work.* Without it, one can easily become disori-
ented in that transitional space, which is much like the shifting
nature of sand between water and land. You've had some practice in examining your self through the windows of experience
and metaphor, so you may already know which questions you
want to pose.

MAKE A list in your journal of six or seven questions you could
ask about your own story. (If you are not sure which questions
to ask, the sample questions in the second bullet above might
give you some ideas.)

Even though you are practicing your role as observer, try to
answer these questions from inside the story. That simply means
we're using both thought *and* feeling: The questions are about
you. Allow them to affect you: Feel the images in the story as
parts of you. Feel the anger, the fear, the poignancy, the peace,
whatever is there. Experience the subtleties of which questions
have more meaning, and allow other questions and associations

to emerge. The observer role helps you to stay honest in examining your experience, to ensure that what's important surfaces.

Taking your time and referring to the questions you listed, write in your journal about what you see through the window of your story's fantasy images.

Consider developing your observer stance by pairing up for a round-two version of this application. (If you don't have the opportunity to pair up, reading this may sharpen your awareness for your own work.) The purpose is to develop a nonjudgmental, observer stance toward fantasy work, as well as to use another person's fantasies for your own discovery and to contribute to theirs. After previewing these guidelines, decide who will be the Storyteller first and who will be the Listener, try it out, and then switch roles.

- Similar to picking up a pen and writing, the Storyteller begins telling a story about anything, for two minutes. The Listener watches the clock and actively listens.

- With gentleness and a spirit of inquiry (not judgment or analysis), the Listener poses some questions for the Storyteller's consideration, like "I wonder what the story might be saying about. . . ."

- The Storyteller responds to the questions and offers any emerging insights about the story; afterward, the Listener offers other possible insights. At this point, the *soul material* of the Listener is inadvertently in the mix: The Listener may pick up on images from the story that reflect the Listener's own inner wilderness. If either partner has feeling toward an insight, positive or negative, it probably has meaning for that person.

- For both partners: The bottom line is to approach the application with mutual vulnerability, respect, and truthfulness.

- Tips for the Storyteller: Give yourself permission to feel somewhat vulnerable, and try to observe the feeling rather than avoid it. It's a clue that you are in that transitional space between the conscious and the unconscious. Also, receive questions or offerings of insight as a gift, letting go of the need to analyze or justify or explain your response. If a suggestion is not helpful, that's okay; others might be.

- Tips for the Listener: Try to hear the story as if it were your story, about you; that will help you to identify meaningful questions for the Storyteller, as well as those relevant to your own inner wilderness. Be mindful to listen with your heart as well as your head, using your own emotional openness to move beyond the rational. And listen to whatever intuitive hunches may emerge.

Now that you've had some practice with fantasy as a window to the soul, watch for opportunities to use it in the work setting. Storytelling is one avenue, especially useful for the practice of allowing fantasy images to emerge, then considering insights from them. As you allow your fantasies to roam, reflect on them. What do you find being reflected back to you? Absurdity, fear, constraint, impulsiveness are all part of the mix in allowing fantasy to bubble up. The material that comes forward is your own personal well of images, and access to these images allows you to better own your own emotional life.

What is your fantasy about that person you talk with regularly but have never met? What is your fantasy about the new proposed restructuring? What is your fantasy about how you are viewed by others? What images from these fantasies serve as clues to your inner wilderness?

Sometimes it's appropriate to share a fantasy with a group, and other times it's not. The story of the empowerment conference and the invitation of the leader to create a fantasy skit helped unlock tension for the entire group. In that situation, group members were asked to consider their fantasies. You may be in a position to ask your group to consider their fantasies, in a situation that feels stuck. Or there may be an occasion where offering a fantasy may seem helpful. There are no rules for when offering a fantasy is appropriate and when not; be aware that the fantasy image may help *you* but could be misunderstood by others. Discretion is advised.

We've explored the inner wilderness of the soul through specific applications that draw on our experience, the use of metaphor, and fantasy. There are, of course, many other ways to actively engage the unconscious—through creative writing, drawing, sculpting, poetry, a dream journal, music, cooking, even doodling.

Everyday situations provide a steady stream of possibilities for exploration of our inner world: What scenes, characters, or images in a movie particularly stir you, either positively or negatively? Did someone say something that struck a nerve with you, and what about *you* is relevant in that event? Were you angered, moved, or entertained by something you saw on the way to lunch? How about that image that went flying through your mind as you started into that meeting? What's that you've doodled on your pad? Images at work might speak to you about your life; images outside of work might speak to you about your work. If you keep a journal, you might start to track what you see that is beyond the visible.

The psyche speaks to us in countless ways, delivering up subtle messages that are clues to the mystery of our own soul. Our greatest challenge is in being still enough to listen.

3

Soul As a Chorus
of Inner Voices

How queer to have so many selves.
How bewildering.

—VIRGINIA WOOLF

IN THE 1920S, English fiction writer Virginia Woolf made a major contribution toward understanding the structure of the personality through her technique of character development. Moving beyond dialogue between people, Woolf brought forward the dialogue within oneself as a way to reveal the inner complexity of a character. Through stream of consciousness, the reader could listen in on the protagonist's interior dialogue. Thus the story shifts to an inner drama, played out among the character's multiplicity of selves. Woolf's appeal, no doubt, stemmed from her readers' recognition of these different aspects within themselves—if not quite the same, similar in their complexity and juxtapositioning. At the time, the popular view of the personality was that of a single, dominant self—an individual who by will could control himself or herself. Woolf and others introduced the idea of many selves, whose voices sometimes harmonize and other times conflict.

In the previous chapter, we used applications to show how using our experience, metaphor, and fantasy can be avenues for identifying and exploring the inner feelings and images that make up who we are. Awareness of how these forces tend to operate in our lives puts us in a better position from which to choose. That is, as we become more aware of what is contained in our inner wilderness, we are better able to bring more of who we are to a particular situation. And that capacity is especially useful for navigating through critical work situations and decisions. In this chapter, we extend that awareness to the idea that familiarity with the multiplicity of selves within nourishes our soul. Learning to recognize and *call up* a particular voice for a particular occasion is a skill that serves as a focus for the chapter.

Identifying Our Multiple Selves

Feelings are key in locating our multiple selves. As a signal function, they point us to the most charged and dynamic elements within. Following the feeling of guilt, for example, could lead us to internal images of authority figures, such as parents, priests, teachers, and all those who have held power over us. We might even imagine these internal figures as speaking particular words— *Steve, you should have followed through on that!*—with a particular tone, and possibly even a certain posture.

As we practice using our feelings to see into the various parts of ourselves, we can learn to observe them in dynamic relation to each other. Which feelings tend to dominate? Which are given the most permission, and which are least allowed? How do they conflict with each other? These questions point to the ways in which feelings, as specific aspects of our selves, can drive our decisions and responses in life. They compete for attention, causing internal conflict and sometimes wreaking havoc when they are not recognized. In contrast with our Western culture's emphasis on rational thought and controlled emotions, acknowledging our feelings is especially important for the journey into our interior world.

Jean is a journalist who feels she lacks the self-worth to do what she wants in her career. In the course of reflecting on her feelings, she has identified two voices that seem continually at odds. One voice is always trying to keep the peace, to appease, and to make her hypersensitive to others' reactions. The second voice is judgmental, alternately angry or critical of others and herself. This voice tends to discount her efforts and dismiss her coworkers. In vying for her attention, these voices often leave her feeling too accommodating of abuse or overly hostile to others. She alternates between being the good girl and taking the fight stance, "Let's get it on."

In having to come to terms with these voices, she named the good girl "Generous Jeanie" and the angry voice "Judgmental Jean." Generous Jeanie is always trying to restrain her opposite instinct, which is to tell people to "screw off," and Judgmental Jean is always trying to admonish her more adaptive side by bitterly putting that side of herself down. "No wonder," Jean tells a friend, "that I can't get anywhere."

In seeking to understand each voice better, Jean has discovered that her anger masks feelings of grieving and sadness and her more accommodating side masks fear of abandonment and a need for approval. But she also has become aware that each voice has been necessary for her survival. A victim of an abusive childhood, Jean sees that the combination of anger and appeasement has allowed her to keep overcoming obstacles but to still conform enough to fit into society and make a living.

When we don't allow a particular feeling to be consciously expressed in our lives, it is likely to express itself anyway—in an unconscious manner, often with unfortunate consequences. For Jean, that meant an internal war that immobilized her. For others, it could mean exploding suddenly in a temper tantrum over something inconsequential. Or it could mean driving ourselves relentlessly, unobservant of our needs, until we finally become sick for three weeks. We are often surprised at such occurrences, whether merely annoying or truly disastrous. In retrospect, of course, we might understand it, but in the moment, we are blind. This is the work of our *shadow* material—those parts of our selves of which we are unaware.

An alternative, of course, is to find a way to allow conscious expression that feels safe.

Cheryl's Story

THE VOICE of the Frightened Girl is not appropriate in most work settings. Yet she is there in me, in particularly stressful situations. When I allow myself to "hear" that voice, I'm less likely to unconsciously act out. And when she's active but I don't recognize her, I can get myself into trouble . . .

- Being late for a meeting
- Not having my notes in order
- Arguing with someone in a tone that says I have to have it my way
- Making someone else small, either in my mind or in words exchanged
- Being confused and unable to keep track of information
- Wanting more support beyond what I really need

It saves me a lot of grief, therefore, if I can keep my antennae up for when the Frightened Girl might be present and I need to hear her out. That is, in a quiet place such as an enclosed office or in the car, I make a conscious effort to listen to what that part of me wants to say, and I connect those feelings to the concerns I'm facing in the work situation. 🐦

In your own stressful experiences at work, which of your selves tends to emerge? Is "he" or "she" the Competitor? the Controller? the Mighty Boss? Which behaviors do you notice that might describe how that voice or aspect expresses itself?

Consciously accessing our different selves and allowing for whatever wants to emerge is a way of paying attention to the myriad of voices that act as counselors within us, each offering a different perspective. Permission for these voices to coexist is one way we honor wholeness. Over time and with gentle guidance, the less desirable aspects of ourselves shift in how much attention they require, making room for new energies to emerge. While internal contradictions are inevitable, the goal is not so much to control as to link together, so the tension of different sides of ourselves eventually connects us to the deeper meaning of our dynamic nature.

Application
IDENTIFYING OUR SELVES AT WORK

We know that a feeling can alert us to a particular aspect of our many selves. Play with the idea that a feeling might lead us to a particular *voice,* and that in that voice is the *expression* of one of our selves. A voice may be made up of one core feeling, or it might actually be the expression of a couple of feelings paired together. For example, "the Judge" might be an expression of certainty and power. Note also that a voice contains both words and tone.

Example by Cheryl: Using the metaphor of the man in the sailboat crisscrossing the channel as an example, one of the things I experienced was feeling critical of myself. Within the feeling of self-criticism was the voice, "Cheryl, you've been zigzagging your way through life just like this guy, changing directions every couple of years. You can't go long enough in one direction to get anywhere. . . ." Within the context of that same experience, I could also speak from the voices of calm or peace, of solitude, of loneliness, and many more. It's as if each voice has its own personality.

In this application, we will use feelings as a way to locate the key aspects of yourself that operate in your work setting, by identifying a voice and the words behind each feeling. Suspending judgment about right or wrong, good or bad, will aid you in moving through this step by step, as will a spirit of playfulness.

REFLECTING ON the experiences you've had at work in this past week, what are some of the key feelings that came up? Try to include the full range of feelings, positive and negative, without trying to pair them (*examples: self-critical, excited, numb, small, fragile, competitive, annoyed*). It will be helpful to list these feelings in your journal.

WHICH FEELINGS are the strongest? Which the most frightening? Note four or five key feelings and any two that seem part of the same experience. (*Example: Small and fragile might come from the same experience, of the child within.*)

IDENTIFY ONE feeling or feeling-pair that might be good to start with. (Pause for your selection.) Imagine that, for right now, you are *only* that feeling. By allowing yourself to shift into that feeling completely, you are bringing it from the past into immediate experience. Listen for the words and tone associated with that feeling—that is, its voice. Imagining how the voice would sound, what are the words which seem to express the feeling? (*Example: Competitive sounds like: Why should he represent us at that conference? I'm the one that mobilized this project, and I know what's going on. Janet trusts me with this stuff more than him. He'll drop the ball. . . .*)

In your journal, you will want to write:

___(Feeling)___ sounds like _____ .

SHIFTING OUT of the last feeling and choosing another, allow yourself to shift again to the immediate experience of this second feeling. (Repeat this process as many times as you wish, taking the time to get into the new feeling completely.) In the voice behind each feeling, write in your journal the words associated with the feeling.

LOOK OVER the feelings you've chosen to work with and the words associated with them. Be mindful of the whole pattern of associations—feelings, words, tone of voice, physical image. Now try to give a name to the part of yourself associated with each feeling-voice-image (*examples: the Competitor, the Controller, the Frightened Girl, the Mighty Boss, the Judge, the Cynic, the Critic*).

These are, essentially, the selves you have identified as active within you in the context of your work. Do you recognize them?

This technique for identifying active aspects of ourselves through feeling, voice, and descriptions (for example, the Competitor) awakens a regard for our inner complexity. Who within us is most active at any given moment? In the first ten minutes of waking up? In a frustrating encounter? In the midst of a boring presentation? We may discover that there are many feelings and voices that can be identified, many—indeed, a plethora—of voices and energies that respond to the question, "Who am I?"

As you are discovering the different voices within you, it may be helpful to keep a few points in mind.

- The different aspects of our multiple selves are there, whether or not we consciously allow them to have voice.

- Acknowledging all of these aspects of our selves puts us in a better position to choose them intentionally. The awareness helps us to see how we're pulled, and that allows us to act from greater awareness, decisiveness, and commitment.

- Each voice has something positive to contribute, and this is related to its reason for existence in the first place. (For example, a self-critical voice may have helped you with some important accomplishments in building your career.)

- The wish to *not* allow a voice is a form of self-annihilation. Not listening for the *minority* selves that are part of you means, simply, that not enough of you is fully available.

- By consciously giving voice to an aspect of ourselves that can be self-destructive, we are practicing the art of self-appreciation. For example, giving space for the self-critical voice to speak allows us to get to know it better. We understand it. We know when it is present. Sometimes it may be important to tell it to pipe down, or at least to wait. We try to acknowledge the good that the voice brings, like attention to quality when that is important. The voice may be destructive if allowed to take over. But in knowing the voice, it is somehow tamed. (See the story of *The Little Prince* in the next section.)

- Any voice, seemingly positive or negative, can be destructive if allowed to go unchecked. (*Example by Cheryl:* There is a creative part of me—my "Creative Woman," I call her. She brings out some wonderful, powerful feelings related to my deepest potentials. If left unchecked, however, she can wreak havoc—the havoc of living by future ideals without pragmatism for today. I may have a lot of fun listening to that voice only, and I might also starve.)

Working with Our Multiple Selves

In the story of *The Little Prince,* a fairy tale for adults, the prince comes upon a fox and invites it to play with him. "I cannot play with you," the fox says. "I am not tamed." The prince asks him several times what that means, and finally the fox responds: "It means to establish ties. . . . To me, you are still nothing more than a little boy who is just like a hundred thousand other little boys. And I have no need of you. And you, on your part, have no need of me. . . . But if you tame me, then we shall need each other. . . . If you tame me, I shall know the sound of a step that will be different from all the others. Other steps send me hurrying back underneath the ground. Yours will call me, like music, out of my burrow."

Then the fox asks the prince to tame him, and the prince declines: "I want to, very much . . . but I have not much time. I have friends to discover, and a great many things to understand." To this, the fox replies, "One only understands the things that one tames."

Finally, the little prince asks what he must do to tame the fox, and the fox instructs him: "You must be very patient. First you will sit down at a little distance from me. . . . But you will sit a little closer to me, every day. . . ."[1]

If we are only willing and take the time, we discover that the uncomfortable parts of ourselves are perhaps not so threatening. Getting to know these different aspects is similar to taming what is wild within us—not so much in the sense of subjugating, which is often how we try to manage those parts of ourselves that we don't like, but taming in the sense of allowing space for familiarity and appreciation. We are developing a relationship to our inner world, a relationship that opens to the fullness of who we are and that leads to ever new discoveries.

A good example of this is Jean, the journalist in our earlier story, who found herself stymied between two competing parts of herself. As Jean came to understand and appreciate each part more clearly, she also learned not to allow them to dominate her life. The taming process, that is, curbed their power over her.

As Jean continues her interior dialogue, she is coming to know another voice that has never been fully acknowledged. She calls this voice "The Referee," and it has been quietly gaining a strength of its own. The Referee is capable of negotiating on behalf of what remains unexpressed in each of her dominant voices. "You want peace," she tells Generous Jeanie in an internal conversation, "but you also have to deal with what makes you angry." And to Judgmental Jean, she negotiates the need for some slack. "You can't just keep tearing up on everything. What's behind the anger?" In this way, Jean has found some freedom to move ahead by first moving sideways, into the voices that keep her stuck.

Like Jean, who took a long time to identify and challenge her internal voices, we may question the value of identifying some of the voices that make us uncomfortable. Isn't there a danger that the voices might become stronger? It would be fine for the positive feelings to become stronger, you might suggest, but what about fear? What about this feeling of self-criticism? To address the question, consider your own experience: What happened as you wrote in the voice of those uncomfortable feelings? Then, *how did you feel about the feeling,* after writing in its voice? You probably experienced something of the power in the voice, in its pure form. Listening to any voice helps us to understand what a powerful impact it can have; and knowing how the voice can serve us helps us to work with it in a more useful way.

Familiarity with our multiple selves does not mean that we can change any of them. Rather, familiarity leads us to greater appreciation for what a voice brings, which enables it to operate in our lives in a more wholesome manner. We can begin to actively choose from the voices we know about, drawing from our own rich inner resources to help us with the occasion at hand.

Application
ATTENDING TO OUR SELVES AT WORK

Review your responses in the last application. Choose the aspects of yourself that you'd like to do more work with, either from among the key feelings you listed or the descriptive names you gave to those feeling-voices.

AS AN observer of your experience, what kinds of circumstances tend to stimulate each feeling into action? When does the voice get active, in other words? (*Examples by Alan:* My Critic tends to get very active when I'm working on something important, especially when I care about what others might think. The Critic whispers "This is poorly done," or "How ridiculous!" My Critic can stop me cold. And my judgmental voice tends to emerge when someone is touching on a subject that is "my area" or that I have strong views about. This voice discounts others and dismisses what is said.) In your journal, you might want to write something like this for each feeling or voice:

(Name of your feeling - voice) appears when _____ .

HOW MIGHT you attend to these feelings? For example, what will be your agreement with your critical voice, or with whatever voices have emerged? (*Examples by Alan:* I will try to bargain with my Critic, to listen to my Critic's voice when it becomes active, during early times in the morning or at the end of a day. During this time it is allowed to express whatever it wishes, uncensored; in exchange, it is quiet while I write or see clients. Also, I'll try to listen to my judgmental voice without necessarily expressing it in conversation. That is, I become aware of my judgmental stance, then try to discern whether it's best to take a stand or keep my mouth shut.)

You can increase your effectiveness by being aware of which of your multiple selves is emerging in a given moment. Imagine what this might look like in your work setting, as you become increasingly aware and practice this skill of working with your multiplicity of selves. You might actively call upon a particular voice for a particular occasion. For example, it might be helpful to call on your Competitor when there are three other businesses proposing to your client. Or perhaps you would want to negotiate with a particular voice when its activity may be problematic. Again using the example of the Competitor, if a colleague is presenting an idea and competing with his or her ideas would be counterproductive, ask your Competitor to quiet down until after the meeting. Afterward, you could write in a private journal in that Competitor voice or simply reflect on the nature of your objections.

Being aware of the circumstances in which a voice is likely to emerge can help you to anticipate its presence and thus work with it, rather than fall victim to it. If you know that competitiveness with your colleagues is an issue, you can go into a team meeting with your antennae up, acknowledging your *feeling* of competition but not allowing it to dominate your behavior. Similarly, in the crossover from your business to personal life, parts of yourself that may work in one context may need to be moderated in another. The Controller might be an appropriate voice for examining progress on a work project, but you might want it to take a back seat when you're having an evening out with your significant other.

As your awareness increases, it can be helpful to recognize when aspects of your selves are teaming up together. For instance, in that proposal to the client, does your Competitor seem to team up with your Critic or your Champion? Imagine the difference that could make! (These names for voices are used as examples; you may already have your own names.)

These voices that have emerged as the energy behind specific feelings are pieces to the puzzle of who you are. Here, the metaphor of an iceberg is appropriate, with only the smaller portion of its mass in visible range. There are many more pieces, many more *selves,* some of which you may not know about consciously until they are given an opportunity to voice their presence.

What is the place inside that can hear all the voices and choose from among them? One image of this ego function is a kind of chair of the board, who can manage the many different selves and decide which one gets the floor. An equally fitting image might be the ringleader of a three-ring circus, who simply points to what is going on. The ability to see and understand, that is, does not necessarily mean control. But operating from a position of higher awareness does enable us to have greater choice within a range of possible actions.

```
           ON HONORING OUR MULTIPLE
              SELVES IN THE WORKPLACE
```

- *Practice sound management: When preparing for an important meeting, consider what aspects of your selves you might call on to lead and which you might ask to not speak.*
- *Bargaining helps: Promise your Critic that after your presentation, you'll take time to listen, and follow through; the critical voice will probably be helpful for the next time.*
- *Be alert for the need to shift: If you are approached suddenly by an upset employee, consider promptly raising awareness to your Empathizer within and, later, perhaps your Problem-Solver.*
- *Be appreciative: When you've gotten through an important situation, what part of you emerged in a way that was especially helpful? You might consciously acknowledge its presence and be grateful. We tend to be quick to criticize ourselves. Why not practice the art of appreciation?*

In a period of stress, it might be helpful to set aside some time to actively reflect on which voices are wanting to be heard. As a meditation, consider writing or even vocalizing these voices. An inquisitive, curious approach is helpful, in which we suspend judgment and allow the energy behind a voice to speak for itself. What does it want you to know?

The journey into soul is a journey of awareness. Standing back for a moment, consider that the complexity of our makeup holds true for others in our work environment. We take this journey along with others. Each of us brings to work a multiplicity of selves, and each of us is somewhere different along the continuum of self-awareness. As sojourners, we are connected: The tensions in each individual soul can be felt as forces in the larger and larger circles of interacting souls. Awareness helps us to honor the different pieces of our selves while they mingle with those of others in our immediate work group and within our organization. This is how we approach the matter of soul in organizations, as a first step. Honoring the multiplicity within moves us toward creating an organization that better reflects the whole human being.

In these three chapters, we examined different meanings of the word *soul;* we ventured into the wilderness of our own soul through experience, metaphor, and fantasy; and we began to dialogue with our multiplicity of selves. Along the way, we applied these matters of soul to the context of work, examining how we can use reflective techniques and awareness of our multiple selves to bring more of the richness of who we are into our work lives. Also along the way, we have probably stumbled into contradictory forces or aspects of our selves we might rather not know about. The chapters ahead will guide us in working with these aspects—to perceive them, to open to the possibility of their hidden gifts, and to integrate them into our personal and professional lives. For the remainder of the book, in fact, the journey of awareness will continue inviting us to weave the connections between our inner world, our work situations, and how we understand ourselves in relation to others and to our work.

4

Shadows
of the Soul

*One does not become enlightened by imagining
figures of light, but by making the darkness
conscious.*[1]

—CARL JUNG

ISTORICALLY, ARTISTS of all types have tended to use movement from darkness to light as symbolic of growth, associating light with the divine. Light represents heaven, knowledge, good, that which is to be sought. *The Great Canon,* composed by St. Andrew of Crete around 700 C.E., celebrates the coming of Christ in the world as symbolized in the appearance of light in the morning and is still sung in monasteries at the break of day. Eighteenth-century artist William Blake chose light and dark figures to represent the struggle between good and evil, with lost innocence portrayed, in one painting, as a child figure reaching toward the sun. An exception to the association of growth with light may have been the Middle Ages, when the events of those times forced people to acknowledge that life is mysterious, that there is much that is unknown, unexplainable. Thus the darkness was valued as an aspect of greatness in the divine—that God was mysterious. But for the most part, light has historically symbolized the ideal.

In contrast, contemporary artist Stephen Schultz presents movement toward darkness as symbolic of growth in consciousness. Suspended between worlds of opposites, his human subjects reach for the unknown. This might be expressed as a painted figure moving toward the edge of the canvas or perhaps gazing into his own dark world.

It is this mystery of the darkness that we are concerned with in these chapters on shadow: What is contained within our own inner darkness? In what ways does the shadow show itself? Why is shadow—our own and others'—relevant to our lives at work? Can we suspend our denial and fear of the unknown long enough to open to some of its mysteries? What, even, can be said with certainty about the shadow?

We all know something about the darker side of life in this society and in the world—the absence of collective responsibility for our educational systems, the expanding divide between the rich and the poor, the advance of AIDS in developing countries, the continuation of so-called ethnic cleansing in various parts of the world. We know about the darker side of organizational life, too—the chaos behind a neatly packaged change effort, the willingness to tolerate destructive behavior as long as profits come in, the silencing of issues that need to be openly discussed. We know, painfully, about some of the darker aspects of our own work life, played out differently for each of us—the dread of going to work in the morning, or the depression on Saturday after a highly stimulating and challenging week; the wear and tear of selling yourself or ideas to others, offered with smiles that disguise the underlying resentment at being in such a position. We know how even in the most glamorous and jet-setting careers, loneliness and boredom can be masked by expensive bottles of Scotch and talk of cigars and foreign hideaways. Clearly, the shadow takes many forms.

The Shadow Bag We Drag Behind Us

What, exactly, is this personal shadow? How did it develop? Robert Bly includes the contributions of Carl Jung and others in his rendition of the shadow:

> When we were one or two years old we had what we might visualize as a 360-degree personality. . . . A child running is a living globe of energy. We had a ball of energy, all right; but one day we noticed that our parents didn't like certain parts of that ball. They said things like: "Can't you be still"? or "It isn't nice to try and kill your brother." Behind us we have an invisible bag, and the part of us our parents don't like, we, to keep our parents' love, put in the bag. By the time we go to school, our bag is quite large. Then our teachers have their say: "Good children don't get angry over such little things." So we take our anger and put it in the bag. . . . Then we do a lot of bag-stuffing in high school. This time it's no longer the evil grownups that pressure us, but people our own age. . . . So . . . out of a round globe of energy the twenty-year-old ends up with a slice . . . [and] the rest is in the bag. . . . We spend our life until we're twenty deciding what parts of ourself to put into the bag, and we spend the rest of our lives trying to get them out again.[2]

We all know about this bag. We may feel its weight, but often we know little about its contents. It makes sense that the contents would seem elusive, because the bag is filled with the aspects of ourselves that we have rejected. Intolerance of these parts of ourselves often runs so deep that we deny their very existence. The consequence of putting different parts of ourselves in the bag is that we limit access to all of who we are.

Gary, for example, is a manager in a travel agency struggling to adapt to major business changes in the wake of e-commerce. Gary has had many ideas for the business over the past several months, but he's had trouble communicating them to his superiors. Before he gets around to talking about an idea with his boss or presenting it in a meeting, it somehow dissipates. Either he finds some reason it won't work, or sometimes he forgets he's even had the idea. When it was pointed out that he seemed to be avoiding the risk of rejection, Gary violently protested—an indication that the suggestion might have some truth. With encouragement, he began to examine this issue until he could see things he'd not been willing to deal with previously.

Gary's fear of rejection seemed, on reflection, to stem from his relationship with his father as a child. Gary couldn't seem to do anything to gain his father's approval. Nothing was good enough, and Gary carried this dread of rejection into his relationship with people in authority, including his boss. It was more tolerable to sabotage his own ideas than to risk rejection. Gary found the pain of longing for approval so intolerable, that he found ways—unconsciously, perhaps—to protect himself from situations where he needed approval.

This is not to suggest that everything is always so black and white. Gary himself pointed out that he did put himself forward at times, that he could, in fact, be a very assertive person. Yet on reflection, he realized that those situations were still relatively safe. Shadow dynamics do not tend to reveal themselves in simplistic ways but more often emerge out of a pattern of behavior.

With new awareness, Gary could consciously approach a situation of risk, anticipate that he was going to be afraid of rejection, and understand why. Instead of backing away from the risk altogether, he could choose to move forward, beyond the fear, into the possibilities. Humor helped. "I guess it won't kill me," he confessed, "if they're not in love with my idea."

Although Gary's new behavior grew out of his insight, his choosing to act differently is what allowed him to shift the pattern. That is, the ability to act in new ways, in addition to insight, allows us to change our habits or behavior. This may seem a subtle distinction, but it speaks to a false assumption that insight alone will allow a person to change behavior. Recognizing the shadow, therefore, is not about only gaining additional insights; it beckons a genuine realigning of our intentions and actions.

An unanticipated benefit to Gary was that once he recognized his fear and put it in perspective, he discovered its positive value. No longer immobilized, he found that some fear actually helped him in his presentations, for it reminded him to anticipate how others would receive his ideas and to consider new ways of communicating them. He has harnessed this childhood wound for positive uses in his life. Perhaps some of the questions in the following application will help to identify what's been assigned to your own shadow bag.

Application
WHAT'S IN YOUR SHADOW BAG?

To discover the pieces of ourselves that are hidden can be challenging. We do it so well, they are truly *hidden*. One way to uncover what we've buried is to imagine ourselves at the age when we actually did the hiding. The questions that follow, therefore, are arranged by the phases of your life and key influences: as a young child and the influence of your parents; as a child in school and your teachers; and as a teenager and your peers. With each question, take the time to picture yourself at that age, to become the child. How big were you? What were you doing? What clothes were you wearing? What did your parent/teacher/ friend look like? The child knows the hiding place and can point to it much more easily than the adult who has picked up this book. Use your journal to record your thoughts, as your responses will be useful later in the application.

REMEMBERING YOURSELF as a small child in your family's home, what are some of the messages/demands about "how to be" that you remember learning from your parents? What did Mommy or Daddy say when you were little, to get you to be good? (*Examples: Good children always look clean and neat. Don't talk back to your mother.*)

WHAT MESSAGES may not have been spoken, but clearly represent lessons you learned from your parents? (*Examples: Don't bother Dad when he's drinking. Don't show weakness.*)

REMEMBERING YOUR early school years, what are some of the messages that you remember learning from your teachers or parents, both spoken and unspoken? (*Examples: It's not nice to tattle. Smiling will get me what I want.*)

REMEMBERING YOUR teenage years, what are some of the messages arising from the viewpoints of your peers? (*Example: Be cool. Don't stand out.*)

Without these *lessons* about life that we picked up from our parents, teachers, and peers, it would be impossible to be integrated into society. Yet there are many opportunities for distortion. The child whose father is drinking may be better off avoiding the potential volatility, but "avoiding conflict at all costs" can become the distorted version that undermines the well-being of the adult.

NEXT, LIST the messages you've identified above in the left-hand column of your journal. For each message, consider ways in which that information has played out in other ways in your life. What might it have led to? What beliefs, values, or judgments about yourself or others do you make, based on that early message? What habits have arisen out of it? Then list what you discover in the right-hand column, writing whatever "I" messages come to mind (see the following example). Be patient and suspend judgment, as much as possible. We're learning to tease out some of the deepest drivers for what we fear, how we think, who we have become.

Original message	Beliefs and habits
"Always look clean and neat."	I never show how confused or angry I feel. I wash my hair before going to the gym. I judge others by how they look.

NEXT TAKE a moment to review what you have listed. Which of those messages, beliefs, or habits seem to have the greatest influence in your life today? Which feel like they are making your bag heavy? Mark them. Then take a moment to consider how these messages have evolved into attitudes and behaviors that you take with you into the workplace. For example: "I can't stand confusion, so I take control before the team has a chance to mess things up."

How has your work life been affected by some of the messages you heard earlier in your life?

Though you have undoubtedly identified beliefs or habits that you might wish to do without, perhaps you've also uncovered early messages that have helped you in your life. For example, being clean and neat may help you to be organized and clear in your thinking; not showing feelings may be appropriate in high-stakes negotiations; not showing weakness may aid you in becoming more self-reliant. Consider all the ways that you have been affected by a certain message that was imposed upon you. Would you trade it all in if it were possible to have escaped its discomfort?

We can begin to see, therefore, how this bag that we carry contains some valuables—"buried treasure" that is essential to the inner work we are describing.

Treasures in the Shadow

Many people fail to find their God-given living water
because they are not prepared to search in unusual

places. . . . One such unexpected source is our own
shadow, that dumping ground for all those characteristics
of our personality that we disown. . . . [These] disowned
parts are extremely valuable and cannot be disregarded.
As promised of the living water, our shadow costs
nothing and is immediately—and embarrassingly—
ever present.[3]

—ROBERT JOHNSON

Shadow elements are not inherently negative. On the contrary, they represent essential, root aspects of our personality, aspects charged with such vitality that they may be mismanaged, misunderstood, and mislabeled. We've seen through the metaphor of the bag how earlier *messages* developed into beliefs and habits that encumber us. Likewise, we can examine this relationship in reverse, starting with our current self-destructive tendencies and looking back to their origins: We find that our destructive tendencies have usually emerged from one of those lessons that we once needed; but the message became distorted, hindering us and adding weight to the bag. By examining the roots of these destructive patterns, therefore, we can discover and reclaim some of the richest, most vital aspects of who we are. And that enables us to bring more of our multiplicity of selves into the work environment in a way that enhances our enjoyment and effectiveness. This task can be daunting. Whatever we have trouble accepting in ourselves, it may seem best to ignore it or to deny its existence altogether. We banish it—to the dark inner world of the unconscious, out of our sight; but in doing so we lose those elements that are like precious stones hidden within the rubble.

John O'Donohue uses the metaphor of the well to speak of the gifts that emerge from the darkness of our inner world:

I often think that the inner world is like a landscape. . . . It is lovely to be on top of a mountain and to discover a spring well gushing forth from beneath the heavy rocks. Such a well has a long biography of darkness and silence. It comes from the heart of the mountain, where no human eye has ever gazed.[4]

In the ancient Celtic world of which O'Donohue writes, wells were considered sacred places, connecting the darker, subterranean world of the unknown with the more visible outer world of light. The land of Ireland was considered to be the body of the goddess, and wells were revered as "special apertures through which divinity flowed forth."[5]

Retrieving the lost treasure buried within the heart of our internal landscape requires a willingness to probe into unexpected, unpleasant areas—into the very roots of our discomforts and our hurts. We are talking about recovery and renewal out of what has been rejected. When properly acknowledged and integrated into our lives, these dark gifts are transformed into our natural strengths.

Two Streams of Gold

There are two common ways that the less desirable parts of ourselves are disowned or assigned to that "not desirable" bin. Both involve rejection but for categorically different reasons. In the first case, we may reject something associated with our early childhood experiences because it is painful. In the second, we reject a greatness, a gift that we refuse to recognize or do not feel we can carry. In either case, if we go back and look at what has been rejected, we can see these parts of ourselves in a different light—not as undesirable baggage, but as lost treasure to be recovered. We could say that these represent two different streams of gold.

Panning for Gold

In this first case, rejecting an aspect of ourselves stems, perhaps unconsciously, from an earlier pain or wounding. We can see that its current manifestation in our lives is dysfunctional. When we consigned it to our inner darkness, it incubated and emerged in a distorted form. It may have had to reappear painfully in our consciousness, to provoke us to come to terms with its existence. The gold in this case is seeing how this rejected aspect has actually served us. When we learn to appreciate its original purpose and consciously integrate that aspect into ourselves, it can come to work more effectively for us rather than against us.

The story of Gary serves as an example of how his avoiding risk was traced back to his longing for his father's approval (a healthy longing) and not receiving it (the wounding). While Gary cannot change the wounding, he can recognize the longing for approval as a healthy aspect of a young boy's need to bond with others and to adapt to the ways of the world. He can also recognize how the fear of rejection can be put to positive use: Rather than avoiding the possibility of his ideas being rejected (a distorted form of longing for connection and approval), he can take steps to minimize the possibility of his ideas being rejected.

Cheryl's Story

EARLIER IN my career, I could not tolerate the fact that I needed more experience to do the things I'd gotten myself into. I started my consulting career with my own private consulting practice, as if I had all the skills I needed. I resisted the notion that I would need to pay the price of years of experience to acquire and know how to use certain tools. The result of my arrogance was a financial crisis, after which I got a job in a consulting firm. Still I did not deal with my inner resistance to needing help.

After a client situation in which it was obvious that more experience would have been beneficial, I realized the need to examine why this issue was so painful to me. I found that it linked back to the awful experience of being a little sister to three big brothers, those guys who had all that experience and who could go out and do anything and bring home trophies. I wanted so much to be older, bigger (as an adult, this meant more experienced). In addition, I saw how the distortion of this element had caused me to discount the experience I did have and how my refusal to acknowledge this need resulted in its destructive expression in my life. Working with the issue has helped me to reclaim the experienced parts of myself, it's led to greater appreciation of the situations which have taught me some lessons, and it's a relief to know that I don't have it all yet. A learner's stance helps me to be open and think creatively, which is valuable no matter how much experience I have. One additional piece of gold is a more general appreciation for having grown up in a family of big brothers; the familiarity with highly competitive environments has enhanced my ability to consult in difficult situations. ❧

Reflection
RETRIEVING WHAT WE'VE REJECTED

Building on the skill learned in the last application, of understanding how earlier messages can lead to dysfunctional habits and behaviors, the exploration in this reflection takes us in the reverse direction. Beginning with what is uncomfortable about ourselves currently, we look backward to its origins and work toward integrating it in a more wholesome way.

The next set of questions require a very different mindset from that of the ordinary, rational world. In a quiet setting, therefore, take the time to make sure you are comfortable and relaxed. Perhaps as you've been reading, you've been reminded of aspects of yourself that you find uncomfortable. Reflect for a moment on what thoughts have come up about yourself. Note whether this is easy to do or troublesome. Keeping in mind that we are probing into difficult material—try to be compassionate with yourself as you move through these questions.

- WHAT IS hardest to tolerate about yourself? (*For example, needing to be the focus of attention, or the tendency to either undermine or inflate your abilities. Perhaps consider a recent experience in which others found you to be difficult in some way.*)

• CHOOSE ONE tendency that stands out and remember specifically the last time that you experienced it. Who was there, what happened? What do you remember thinking? Saying? Feeling?

Next, try to remember when you might have experienced this same tendency in an earlier period of your life, perhaps in a slightly different way. Reflecting very slowly, try to remember or imagine an even earlier time. And an earlier time. Trust that your imagination, if not your memory, will lead you to the most essential parts of who you are.

• WHERE DOES your reflective imagination take you? Has it led you to an earlier experience or situation? What seems to be the original reason for this tendency?

Take a moment to acknowledge how this tendency served you in its earlier time. Then slowly bring your thoughts back to the present, observing how the distortions have dominated your present behavior.

• WHAT WILL you do with this new awareness? How might this tendency be modified, so that it serves you and others better?

Consider recording some of your thoughts in your journal, while they are fresh.

So much of what we have been hiding in the bag we drag behind us, we find, upon examination, is related to our vitality. Paradoxically, many of our defensive habits (stubbornness, acquiescence, sarcasm) stem from the same painful experiences that formed positive aspects of our personality (our tenacity for justice, our gentleness of spirit, our sensitivity to others, or our humor). Whatever it is about ourselves that has been so difficult to accept, its origins can usually be traced to some of the most precious, essential elements of our makeup. The challenge is to move from hiding and ignoring it to finding its value in our lives. We shouldn't be too hard on ourselves, for this shift requires courage, patience, and compassion. Slowly, our appreciation for what has been undesirable grows and our range of choices for expressing it expands. This is what it means to integrate it back into our lives in a more wholesome way.

Standing in Our Glory

The second stream of gold involves a more subtle form of rejection: Aspects of who we are become relegated to shadow by rejecting a greatness for which we do not wish to be responsible. This could be a talent, a gift, or some aspect of our beauty as a person. Greatness can be overwhelming, either in terms of how it sets us apart from others or because of the inherent responsibility that accompanies it. Our unconscious response might be to *hide our light* through any number of ways of avoiding or discounting ourselves, thus banishing the gift into the hidden recesses of our shadow. The shadow expression, therefore, might be a denial of the gift or an internal force that criticizes or diminishes it or that arranges circumstances so that its potential is never realized. The gold is in seeing how this gift need not be embarrassing or cumbersome. We can learn to appreciate our gift and stand in its greatness.

Nelson Mandela spoke to this tendency of hiding of our gold when he read from Marianne Williamson in his inaugural address:

Our deepest fear is not that we are inadequate. Our deepest fear is that we are powerful beyond measure. It is our light, not our darkness, that most frightens us! We ask ourselves, who am I to be brilliant, gorgeous, talented, fabulous? Actually, who are you not to be? You are a child of God. Your playing small does not serve the world. There is nothing enlightened about shrinking so that other people will not feel insecure around you. We are all meant to shine as children do. We were born to make manifest the glory of God that is within us. It's not just in some of us, it's in everyone. And, as we let our own Light shine, we unconsciously give other people the permission to do the same. As we are liberated from our own fear, our presence automatically liberates others!

There are so many different ways that our gifts might be manifest, whether inwardly or outwardly. Likewise, there are just as many ways to hide what is extraordinary about ourselves. The tendency to hide our gifts is especially great in work settings where there is pressure to conform to others' expectations of us.

At forty, Ben was the senior psychologist of a state mental hospital who ran a nationally recognized program for the treatment of schizophrenics, had published two books, and headed a lecture series that brought luminaries together from around the country. Ironically, he never had great faith in his own ideas. His talent, he believed, was in facilitating the great ideas of others, and he dismissed even the suggestion that he had any original ideas of worth. As a result, he struggled with feelings of inferiority. He was not able to account for his own contribution and could imagine being easily replaced. Later in life, Ben came to realize that his gift lay in his ideas about leadership and innovation—ideas that had not been expressed by others. The discovery of this gold enabled him to express his ideas more freely. Ben began to speak out more, becoming an advocate for organizational innovation as well as a support for people who doubted the value of their ideas.

Alan's Story

I REMEMBER A meeting I had with my graduate professor, a woman who was to become my mentor for organizational consulting. In a conversation we had, I complimented her on her ability to use her feelings of anger constructively in groups— being direct, but never insulting. To my surprise, she confronted me. She told me, without mincing words, that I, too, had this gift, of being able to understand and use my own feelings, but that I wasn't using it appropriately. She pointed out that I often hid my feelings and acted out sarcastically toward people who upset me. I remember that I was shocked and disturbed by her confrontation; yet the sting of her words incited me to be aware of how I worked with my feelings in groups. The suggestion that I had a gift pushed me toward greater responsibility in using it. Attempting to be more self-aware of my sarcasm, I was freer to attend to the emotions of others. ❧

Reflection
RECOVERING OUR GREATNESS

In a quiet, comfortable setting, reflect on the talents, gifts, and sources of vitality associated with who you are. Notice whether this is easy for you to do, or whether it's difficult. Take your time in considering the following questions, and apply them as appropriate to your work situation.

- WHAT IS it that you feel especially proud of? In what ways have you been recognized by others that have really touched you?
- WHAT TALENT or gift do you feel most reluctant to express?
- CAN YOU remember a time when you felt embarrassed about something positive about yourself?
- ARE THERE specific areas of discomfort that lead you to want to hide aspects of who you are, such as physical beauty, analytic intelligence, humor, or intuition?
- CONSIDERING THE preceding questions, which one aspect seems most diminished or suppressed in your life?
- WHAT CHOICES might you make about standing in your own greatness? How might you bring this gift to your work?

It's important to examine how we have dealt with our own gifts. Have we inflated them or devalued them, perhaps in the hopes of making others more comfortable with us? Do we mask our physical beauty with unattractive clothing, or do we flaunt it or distort it? Do we inflate our intellectual gifts, or do we devalue them, not wanting to stand out? Do we allow our feelings to be seen by others, to be used as a gift to others? Do we disguise our longing for connection, with a persona that screams "Independence!"? How do we use our talents? our humor? our grace? our intuition?

This is not to say that hiding our gifts is entirely our own doing, as in Gary's case of hiding his ideas to avoid rejection. Occasionally the social roles we are in simply do not allow us to exhibit our gifts. An all-too-familiar example is the woman who feels that she must mask her thoughts and feelings in the workplace—often an extension of a social role in the family that did not permit her to be the intelligent one or to directly challenge norms about power. A parallel example would be the man who refuses to show emotions and must appear at all times to be in control. Clearly, the social roles in our family and work structures have a great deal to do with which of our gifts we feel are permissible and which we feel are not. These are things we negotiate throughout the course of our lives, attempting as adults to place ourselves into the environments most favorable to our inner complexity.

As you may have discovered already in moving through this chapter, shadow material is a bit like a house of mirrors. No sooner do we think we understand something about ourselves than we are confronted again by new distortions and new reflections. In working with shadow, we see a continual interplay of the mystery of who we have been and who we are seeking to be. Because it is so complex, pervasive, and essential to our growth, the next two chapters continue a discussion of the shadow. In chapter 5, we examine the shadow in our interactions with others and in everyday work situations, and in chapter 6, we explore ways of living with and even cultivating a relationship with our darker side.

5

Playing with Wild Cards

When we begin working on our own souls, we
discover that we are not self-made. Our identity
depends on Another. We cannot make ourselves . . .
but fortunately a wild card has been announced.[1]

—ALAN JONES

I<small>T'S IMPOSSIBLE TO</small> recover the lost pieces of ourselves in isolation. It takes bumping into a lot of difficult situations and people to find out who we really are, and for this the workplace setting is ideal. Consider the surprise at the impact of another person on our lives. This wild-card "other" might take the form of a mentor, whose loyalty is unquestionable and whose insights have solidified our own sense of competence, or of an irritating coworker, whose only perceived value may seem to be in teaching us patience. The wild-card other may be encountered in the form of a stranger on the street who ignites our emotions, or a stranger within our own home—the spouse or child whose behavior or outlook seems painfully alien. Whether experienced as positive or negative, an encounter with this other often leads to insight and growth.

Cheryl's Story

WALKING INTO the second-semester class of Organization Behavior in my graduate program, I was furious at what I saw. Sitting in the spot of the female Hispanic professor I had grown to trust and respect was, instead, "yet another white male." She had left the program for a consulting position, it was announced, and he would be replacing her. Over the course of the semester, I slowly let go of the resentment and came to appreciate the new professor's competence and genuineness. Now, a decade after having so easily dismissed him, I count him as the single greatest source of learning for me in consulting to organizations. Because of this initially unwanted *other*, I discovered several unrecognized aspects of myself, such as a capacity for prejudice and a desire for authenticity in the consulting relationship. ❧

Through these encounters with the other, our identity takes shape: *You are strange to me, different. It is in contrast with who you are that I have a sense of who I am.* Our own beliefs and preferences take on meaning as they are differentiated from those of others. The other, in a less personal sense, might also appear in the form of a situation that sparks a strong reaction. *That idea is repulsive, one that I would never propose.* Or, *That is unquestionably the right decision, one that everyone should agree to.* As we bump up against people and circumstances, we come to identity ourselves by what we like and dislike.

Similarly, our shadow has a lot to do with how we *don't* want to identify ourselves. We prefer to see it *out there* instead. That is why certain difficult encounters, with people or initiatives, can spark such enormous energy—energy that cannot be accounted for rationally: We project it outward, because there is such a strong need to see it *out there* rather than own it within. Thus the person or situation becomes a projection screen for our own material. By reflecting on our reactions to people and events, therefore, we can learn something about what we do not tolerate within ourselves.

THE WILD-CARD OTHER WITHIN

Just as there is an other out there, so there is a wild-card other within—a shadow aspect that pops out from behind its cover to confront us. Failing to acknowledge the unwanted parts of ourselves is analogous to the alienation of living with a stranger in our own home, and continued refusal to address this stranger is like banishment or even internal psychic murder. On the other hand, should we find the courage to turn and face the stranger with openness and curiosity, rather than in judgment, we would no doubt develop deeper appreciation for the unique gifts this part of our personality brings to our lives. Jung wrote, "The 'other' within us always seems to us strange and unacceptable. But if we allow ourselves to be affected and hurt by it, then it goes into us, and we are the richer for a piece of self-knowledge."[2] This goes to the heart of how vulnerability, our capacity to experience uncomfortable aspects of ourselves, leads to self-knowledge. Can we be richer for considering aspects of our own personality that we are rightly concerned with—our rigidity, our lust, our thirst for revenge? The answer is a cautious "yes."

In this chapter, we explore the nature of our reactions and how they might serve as indirect avenues into the shadows of our soul. We discover just how pervasive the shadow is, present in every interaction. Consequently, we see how inside-out our conscious views may be—that things are not always as they appear. When taking into account our shadow selves, we discover the intermingling of "good and evil"—that our good intentions may not be so pure and that unfortunate circumstances may lead to some worthy outcomes. Understanding the nature of shadow in interactions is our best hope for making sense of the tensions between people and the explosion of events at work.

Reacting to the Wild Card

One of the indirect ways we can approach our shadow is to examine whom we admire and why we admire them, whether real people or fictional characters. And sometimes what we learn can be surprising.

Alan's Story

PAULA, A Quaker by background, had spent the last year learning to navigate as a senior manager in her division. Today we had agreed to talk about what values seemed most prominent during the good and tough periods of her past year. Was there anything she learned about herself? She paused for a moment and asked me if I'd ever seen *Gone with the Wind*. Looking very serious, Paula told me she loved the character of Scarlett. "Why?" I asked. "Because she's such a conniving bitch." Taken aback, I asked her to say more. Paula explained that Scarlett has no value system, at least not one that could be respected. "She is manipulative to the bone, even when she is acting innocent. But she is what she is, no sham about her. She is so fresh and so beautiful." And being dramatic for effect, Paula declared, "I would give it all up to be that beautiful."

The way Paula relished speaking of Scarlett was moving, for this character so clearly stood for something opposite of Paula's own traditional value system. I was also moved by what Paula admired about Scarlett—her beauty, her utter clarity about getting what she wanted, her skill at manipulation, her freshness, and her being who she really is. It seemed these latter qualities, albeit through a distorted mirror, described Paula. Over the course of the past year, she had embraced her role as political, particularly in dealing with other divisions and the corporate office. She knew that getting things done meant understanding others' agendas and creating coalitions. She also had become increasingly savvy about manipulating her budget and encouraged her direct reports to do the same. And she was never reluctant to be "innocent," asking for help or seeking clarification at strategic points. Paula, it seemed to me, delighted in getting her way, though she was a woman of utmost integrity. No sham or pretense about her. ❧

Paula's capacity to claim Scarlett as a *friend (other)*, regardless of how utterly opposite they might seem, allowed her to also claim the gold that sparkled in this manipulative character.

Reflection

DISCOVERY THROUGH OUR POSITIVE REACTIONS

Perhaps as you've been reading, you've already remembered a movie character with whom you've strongly identified. If not, take a moment to reflect back through the years, remembering any movies that have attracted your interest in an exceptional way. In this movie that has always attracted you, what character has lingered in your imagination? Imagine this character in one of your favorite scenes.

- WHAT DID you especially admire about the character? What were his or her strengths?
- IN WHAT ways are the character's strengths and flaws related?

Take a moment to consider the impact this character has had on you.

- CONSIDER THAT your reactions to this character are to some extent reflections of what is present within you, perhaps in a less obvious way. Which aspects of the character you admire are you able to recognize within yourself?
- IN WHAT ways do you express these admirable qualities through your work?

• As you've pondered these questions, does your identification with the character on the screen suggest any issues you are wrestling with internally?

Alan's Story

WHEN I was a teenager, I watched Clint Eastwood westerns—*Hang 'Em High, A Fistful of Dollars, For a Few Dollars More,* and *The Good, The Bad, and The Ugly.* One day I watched all four of these films in one seating. Later, in my twenties, I remember hitchhiking to visit a friend in New Mexico, buying a cigar, smoking it down to its nub, and knocking on his door wearing a poncho. Eastwood's character was called the man with no name and I somehow identified with this amoral loner whose motivation was often revenge. Yet I recognize also the toughness, willingness to go it alone, and a decency and sense of justice this character stood for. This was a man not to be messed with, a man who had nothing to lose, and a man who therefore could not be manipulated by others. These characteristics remain today important attributes of my internal landscape. ❧

Our positive reactions to others, whether people in movies or people at work, are indicators of our inner gold. When you stop to think about it, this is a remarkable point. It means that every time we find ourselves admiring someone, we are admiring a piece of ourselves somewhere within. This is true regardless of whether we are conscious of the link. Were there no elements in our internal makeup reflecting what is out there, we simply would not notice those particular things to which we react. Usually it is the case that the stronger the reaction, the more hidden this element is to us: In other words, a reason something may be so strongly identified *out there* is because we are not yet conscious of that quality *in here.* Once we identify its presence within, the reactions diminish in their intensity, because we no longer need to project it out.

Discovery Through Our Negative Reactions

Working with a negative reaction to an other requires a bit more courage than working with our positive reactions, although the principles are the same. When we become annoyed at someone, impatient, disgusted, or judgmental, we can know that, somewhere within, there is a *piece of our own* that corresponds to what we find difficult *out there*.

Cheryl's Story

A T A retreat I attended on the shadow, participants were required to watch some, shall we say, unpleasant films. Whether featuring serial killers or modern-day vampires or colonial conquest, each film offered up a different flavor of stress for me. The instructor asked us to pay attention to our reactions, noting which characters we especially disliked or feared or admired. Annoyed but stuck, I resolved to participate as openly and wholeheartedly as possible.

The first film was *The Mission,* about the impact of colonial conquest on missions among native populations in South America. Perhaps the most remarkable lesson I took from that film was through the debriefing afterward: It seemed each viewer had favored a different character, and each had despised a different character—and not the ones I would have thought to be obvious. As the instructor probed and participants explained their reactions, the internal makeup of participants was revealed with each pleasant or troubled response.

Perhaps the most difficult film for me was *The Hitcher*— a chilling thriller in which a serial killer relentlessly pursues a college-age boy—not to kill, but to torment him with fright. In desperation for his life and the circumstance of being framed for the killer's murders, the boy takes on more and more behaviors of the killer, until his innocence is completely overcome and he is able to kill the serial killer himself. My reactions to the story seemed to be related to the often dogged pursual with which I go after the unconscious parts of myself, routing out what hides in the dark in a relentless attempt to shed light and understanding on those areas—so much so that my conscious ego can become a kind of tormentor that chases after my innocence. I've learned from this to be more patient with myself, more sensitive to the pacing of my own psychological understanding—that some things need more time. ❧

The next time you attend a film, pay attention to the characters you like and dislike and points of action when you felt your strongest reactions. You can use these observations to ponder what the movie may be reflecting back to you.

As you think about a movie character that you have found troublesome, what does that character tell you about your other within?

The term *projection* refers to the principle that whatever we have trouble identifying as within ourselves (positive and negative), we identify as belonging to someone else. Consider the possibility that every reaction is a projection and, therefore, begins within. *My coworker dresses so meticulously—who is he trying to impress?* Whether I dress sloppily or neatly, the principle of projection would suggest that I actually care a great deal about how I look myself, not just about how my colleague looks, though I may not like to think of myself as being concerned with appearance. The stronger the reaction, the more likely it is that something within does not want to come out of hiding—thus the preference for seeing it in someone else, as justification that "I'm not like that." To *work a projection* is to make the links between what we see out there and what is within—by noting our reactions, seeing how it may be true for ourselves, and accepting that "this, too, is me."

Application
Taking Back a Projection

For every finger pointing out, there are three pointing back. This application is designed to help us work a projection—to own it, to take it back into ourselves. Starting with the finger pointing out, we move toward the fingers pointing back, examining what the reaction might be saying about ourselves. For this application, therefore, imagine that you react *only* because there is something already in your internal makeup that is similar, and try to suspend judgment as you move through the steps and record your responses in your journal.

1. Identify a strong reaction you've recently had to a person or an event. (*Example: Steve comes off as being so together— always smiling, energetic, prepared in his plans or for his presentation. I can't stand it! I just don't trust him, that he's for real. He doesn't seem human.*)

2. Point the finger: "You are so. . . ." or "That is so. . . ." Feel the emotion. (*Example: "You are so perfect! Don't you ever need help from anyone?!"*)

3. Identify when you have experienced that emotion before, earlier in your life. (*My older sister seemed to be good at everything she did; achievement came naturally. For me, any accomplishment seemed to take a lot more effort. I remember being angry about this sometimes.*)

4. Identify how you may have been this way toward someone else. (*Others have told me that I can be hard to get to know, that I come across as independent. I think my tendency is to present my best side and hide any feelings of insecurity or needing others.*)

5. Identify when you have been this way toward yourself. (*Sometimes I'll get deeply into a piece of work before realizing I could use some help. I want so much to do it on my own that I will convince myself that I know what I'm doing.*)

Learning from the Wild Card

With practice at examining our reactions as indicators of our shadow, we are able to move more deeply into the hidden meanings behind our reactions, our lesser-known motives for doing what we do, or our protective reasons for having certain values. Not all is what it may appear to be at first glance. Some values inherently conflict with others; yet it is important that they coexist. This deeper level of examination takes great patience, requiring us to suspend justification for our reactions, actions, or beliefs. It requires that we remain open, inquisitive as to what could emerge out of hiding. In the fast-paced work environment, this is especially difficult. The collective values of the workplace shout that we should be decisive, take action quickly, and not reveal ambiguity.

The story of Henry provides us with a good example of learning from a "wild card" dealt to him at work. Henry is a nurse practitioner in a medical clinic that encourages close working relationships between physicians and other care providers. One innovative strategy within the practice was to have physicians and nurse practitioners pair up and "shadow" each other while seeing patients.

Henry paired up with Dr. Thomas, the physician he most admired and who, with Henry, had championed this shadowing strategy to others. To Henry's horror, however, he found one of Dr. Thomas's practices abhorrent—that he would routinely put on gloves before seeing each patient. How could he, in a time of fear and misinformation about AIDS, further the stereotype that touch is dangerous? How could he be so old-fashioned?

Although the patients themselves did not seem to mind, Henry felt this action violated what was right.

Henry lost confidence in Dr. Thomas, questioning even whether he wanted to continue working with him. Other practitioners Henry talked with in confidence dismissed the idea that this was a serious problem. Yet Henry's feelings grew more troubled. He could not imagine addressing his concern to Dr. Thomas without being somehow offensive. We know shadow forces are at play when we are left reeling by an unanticipated event. What irony, that this well-intentioned program to shadow each other had turned so dark.

Without the ability to step back and examine our reactions, the negative feelings evoked are overwhelming. To Henry's credit, he was willing to reflect on what occurred, to see how his reaction was rooted in his own personal trials. In the end, Henry planned to talk with Dr. Thomas. But perhaps more important, the event lost its emotional charge as Henry came to understand more consciously his own strongly held beliefs and how a valued colleague might act differently than himself.

Also to Henry's credit, he was aware that true collaboration could not take place without differences arising. Henry even used the metaphor of this event being "fertilizer" for some new growth that might occur. Shadow material, very much like fertilizer, is what we have to work through in order to grow and move on.

Unless we are practiced in pausing to reflect when faced with such a difficult situation, we are more likely to *react* impulsively than to *respond* thoughtfully. Henry could not have moved through this experience as he did without asking himself a number of penetrating questions. Consider taking time now to examine a presently difficult situation in your work life, using the *Strategic Questions for Uncomfortable Encounters*. Or make note of where this is in the book, so that when a future opportunity arises, you can return to these questions easily.

STRATEGIC QUESTIONS FOR UNCOMFORTABLE ENCOUNTERS

In a quiet setting, consider the dilemma troubling you. Try to let go of all judgment regarding your responses, open to the possibility of insight through this wild card, and reflect on the following questions.

• *What is it about this situation that's troubling to you?*

> • *What is most surprising to you about this situation?*
> • *What seems most difficult for you to accept about it?*
> • *What reactions to others are you having?*
> • *Do you find yourself needing to go beyond your normal modus operandi to resolve the dilemma? In what ways do you feel personally stretched or challenged?*
> • *As you reflect on this situation, what insights come up about the other within?*

Dealing with shadow contents and how we judge others requires a certain degree of vulnerability—a willingness to "melt," which may be a key toward revealing the things we most treasure and care about. Henry realized how deeply he cared about people understanding that they do not need to be afraid of touch. But to find this gold, he had to first judge a deeply admired colleague and fear that their relationship was destroyed. There is something poetic, paradoxical, about this alchemy of the shadow—that from the baser instincts (fear, judgment, self-righteousness), we have the capacity to find something that offers us greater wholeness.

The Subtleties of Good and Evil

Sharon was a specialist in the order fulfillment process of her company and was asked to be a member of the redesign team. She was initially very excited, for the redesign was to be based on principles of empowerment—that those who are closest to the work know how to do it best and should design the work. But after a few meetings, Sharon sought help. "Yes, we're doing our own analysis," she said of the employee-only design team, "and we know what the problems are, and we know how best to fix them." She struggled to find her next words. "The trouble is, our solution for redesign is *not* going to give people more say in how they do their work. It's going to take away from some people the responsibility for certain decisions that will now be carefully scripted—credit decisions, for instance. So those of us on the design team might be having our say about how things ought to be done—but empowerment in the workplace? It's just not gonna happen. Credit reps will be making fewer decisions themselves, and they'll be angry."

At first glance, one might identify a program such as "empowerment" as positive: A key principal of empowerment is that individuals who are closest to the work will have greater say in how the work gets done. Yet, Sharon feared the negative outcome of their empowerment efforts—that her colleagues would actually be *less* empowered. A closer look often reveals the interplay of positive and negative—or "good" and "evil" within a single situation. Consistent with our exploration of shadow, its treasures, and the wild-card other, seeing the complexity of good and evil enables us to soften our judgments. We become more tolerant of others and more alert to our own blindness. As we move forward through this section, we'll examine how good can contain evil and how evil can contain good, shifting the attention increasingly toward examining this phenomenon within ourselves.

A NOTE ABOUT GOOD AND EVIL

Evil here is imagined as the darker side of human nature, the degrees to which we are willing to harm or destroy whatever seems to be in the way of our own needs and urges for power, domination, and self-interest.

Good here is imagined as that higher capacity of human nature to recognize and serve others according to virtuous principles of caring, justice, healing, and mutual benefit. The authors work with the premise that we are, as a whole, less good than we imagine ourselves to be and not as evil as we may fear.

Etymological note: The word evil *appears to come from the English and German root word meaning* excessive; *thus, whatever becomes excessive (or one-sided) increases the capacity for evil.*

There seem to be multiple paradoxes present with regard to the interplay of good and evil. Feelings of fragmentation coexist with possibilities for wholeness. Similar to the relationship of a sweet fruit with its bitter skin, we might say that the seeds for wholeness are found *within* the hard, bitter circumstances of the dilemma. Only through the willingness to work with such base emotions as fear, judgment, and self-righteousness are we able to break through to more creative alternatives. To work with conflicting emotions and outcomes, we need patience and a willingness to move toward wholeness.

Fifteenth-century artist Berthold Furtmeyer portrayed a similar paradox of the holding together of opposites—creativity and destruction. In *Tree of Life and Death,* the tree of knowledge rises up from Adam's belly, while two women stand beside the tree, passing out fruit—one, to a line of people for their salvation, and the other, to a line of people for their damnation. Fruit from the tree of creativity (life) is also fruit from the tree of destruction (death).

Cheryl's Story

THE SMALL town I grew up in—Herculaneum, Missouri, on the Mississippi River—was originally founded as a company town. This meant that years earlier the lead plant had owned all the houses and the general store. The idea was to attract workers by providing for their daily needs. (The reality was that workers had little choice with regard to employment.) Workers received these provisions, of course, in exchange for submitting to dangerous, dirty, smelly, and exhausting working conditions. From the same company came both resources for living and obstacles to enjoying life. ❧

In today's work environment, we find the mixture of simultaneous opposites at times confusing. It would not be uncommon today to find a management development program built around empowerment while pink slips are being handed out for the next round of downsizing. The image of the fruit from the tree reminds us that our actions can take on opposite meanings. At a time of such fast-paced change and the inevitable destruction of former ways of doing things, we need the inner resources for dealing with issues of ambiguity. The alternative is to be paralyzed or to make rash judgments.

The red flag here is to be alert to the possibility of the opposite. Sharon learned to be alert to the unintended negative outcomes that were inherently built into the empowerment program. And, to the other side of the equation, the workplace offers plenty of difficult situations in which to practice looking for the possibility of good.

Andrew had been the CEO of a marketing firm for two years, when one day, out of the blue, the CEO of the parent company paid him a visit and fired him. Apparently their biggest client simply didn't like Andrew, end of story. Stunned, he and his wife panicked at the financial implications, with three teenagers approaching college. But he decided that, rather than seeking other employment, this was an opportunity for him to establish himself. Working from home, Andrew began writing at 4:00 each morning and developing his network of contacts during business hours. He and a partner set up a consulting practice, and within a few months he was getting invitations to speak to marketing groups. Ten years later, Andrew's fourth book is a best-seller, his firm has offices in four continents, and he's been featured on magazine covers. Though initially he felt a deep humiliation at having been fired, Andrew now concedes that this wild-card event propelled him into the greatest period of creativity and productivity he's ever experienced.

The workplace is rife with similar stories, of "good programs" leading to unintended difficulties and of "bad events" leading to unexpected breakthroughs. Efforts to have everyone come together as a team can expose how superficial people really are and how disjointed they are from each other. A merger driven by financial necessity and forced on people can bring to the surface new creativity. It may seem obvious that any single event would simultaneously contain elements of good and evil. Yet how great is the tendency to identify ourselves completely with one side or the other! This seems especially true when these events concern us directly. What we imagine to be so positive can, with enough contradictions, become seen as rotten to the core.

Acknowledging the double-sided nature of events, therefore, is fundamental to wholeness in the workplace. And because it is so contrary to our one-sided tendencies, it requires an intentional focus. Sharon was able to ease her colleagues' disappointment with workforce empowerment and the redesign, not with an effective communication campaign boasting its merits, but by honestly examining both sides of the issue and presenting them as *dilemmas* to be contended with. Andrew was able to recover from the humiliation of being terminated by asking himself such questions as, *What can I learn from this? What opportunities can I discover through this difficulty?* and *How can I turn my fear into positive energy?*

Reflection
FINDING THE POSSIBILITY OF GOOD

In a relaxed setting, consider a work situation that you have thought of as predominantly negative. Take a moment to experience, or to *feel,* all of the negative emotions you've had toward this situation. Without trying to move ahead in this reflection, acknowledge the negativity with which you've viewed this situation.

- ASSUMING THAT you are justified in your negative judgments, what are they?

Breathing slowly and deeply, as you inhale, acknowledge the one-sidedness with which you tend to view the situation. As you exhale, try to let go of all of your judgments for the time being. (They will be there later. For now, we want to start with an empty slate on this situation.) In a spirit of openness, consider that there are some positive things to be gleaned from this situation, though you may not know what they are. When you feel ready, reflect on these questions.

- In what ways are you challenged by this situation? Where are you being stretched?

- As a result of either knowing about this situation or experiencing it directly, personally, what is there for you to learn?

- What are you most afraid of or angry about? How can you use that emotion for constructive purposes? Or how might you use the energy of that emotion in a different way?

- What could happen positively as a surprise result, in spite of how negatively this situation has been set up? for yourself? for others?

Reflection
Finding the Possibility of Evil

Now consider a work situation that you have thought of as predominantly positive or good—perhaps a project you are involved in or a decision you are about to make. Take a moment to feel all of the positive emotions you've had toward this situation. Acknowledge the strength of just how positive your perspective is.

- What feelings do you have?

Again, breathe slowly and deeply. As you inhale, acknowledge the one-sidedness with which you tend to view the situation. As you exhale, try to let go of all of your positive judgments for the time being. Consider the possibility of some negative consequences arising out of this situation, though they may be unintended. When you feel ready, reflect on these questions.

- What difficulties or negative outcomes could develop out of this situation, in spite of its plan or how it is communicated? Could others be harmed? misled? disappointed?

- To what extent are these outcomes recognized by others, or to what extent do they tend to be glossed over?

- WHAT ARE some possible ways you can honor both sides while addressing the problematic aspects of this situation?

Perhaps, in the course of working through this material, you've already identified a time you were surprised with negative outcomes of good intentions. We have all been vulnerable to this phenomena, of acting out of our *best intentions,* only to have something backfire in our faces! Embarrassed and baffled, we can do little but mumble about having had good intentions— "Really!" Similarly, we have all been on the receiving end of someone else's good intentions toward us, when our experience was entirely different, ranging perhaps from bewilderment to anger. Truly, we can know that the Trickster-Other is at work, when out from behind the billboard of good will pops disappointment, chaos, or betrayal.

Frank was a young, bright manager who had been promoted faster than any of his peers. Still in his thirties, he was tapped to take charge of a key but troubled department within the company. As he took up his leadership role, he cited as one of his strengths the willingness to offend people if necessary. The department, he believed, suffered from avoiding tough issues. His intention was to confront these issues, including that of fairness among senior and junior employees, especially as it related to the distribution of assignments. As department head, he had the big picture and the right answers.

In less than a year, Frank was forced to take a reassignment. The only thing his troubled department could agree on was that Frank was not the right person for the job. Many liked him, but he had offended so many of them that no one felt he had the credibility to lead. Fairness had become an excuse for nearly everyone to complain they were being treated less fairly than someone else. Frank's attempt to resolve the problems resulted in his appearing imperial, alienating the senior members of the department and intimidating the junior employees. And the actual distribution of assignments turned out to be far more complicated an issue than Frank had ever anticipated.

Frank was hurt by his reassignment but found in it reason to reflect on his good intentions. "I thought that by confronting people and getting the job done, I would be appreciated overall. I realize now that, although there was progress, I undermined any chance for future support on working the tough issues. My values are not necessarily everyone else's. And that's a lesson I'll be able to use."

It is exactly in such circumstances involving our best intentions that we are most vulnerable to shadow—most *in need* of course-correcting by a wild card. To the extent that we are convinced our actions are only for the good, an ambush surely awaits. One might ask, Why should this be so? Why should our good intentions not be taken at face value? While there is no clear and direct answer to this phenomenon, we can only point out that the shadow loves to hide behind what seems obvious. It is as if the bright sunlight cast upon a tree causes the darkness of its shadow to be that much more concealing. Best intentions, rigid values, and things with which we strongly identify all express ways that we tend to idealize—hence the usual pattern of one-sidedness and the shadow's tricks that force us to reckon with the dual-sided nature of things. Provided that we can humble ourselves enough to obtain forgiveness for our shortcomings and recover from the initial trauma of surprise, perhaps we can also appreciate a bit of the irony: After all, it is usually for our own good, in the end, that we would have endured the wild-card shenanigans.

We are concerned here with building the capacity, or the skills, for examining the dual-sided nature of events that come our way. This is the essence of soul work—gathering up the pieces of ourselves and holding opposite forces in tension long enough for new creative possibilities to emerge. To the extent that we practice these skills systematically, we are better prepared to respond spontaneously when the demands arise.

STRATEGIC QUESTIONS
FOR OUR BEST INTENTIONS

In a quiet setting, think about a pending situation representing good intentions on your part. If the situation has already occurred, use this as an opportunity to deepen your understanding or to follow up with other actions. Recognizing that your own actions have their double-sided nature (as do everyone's), open to the possibility of greater awareness regarding your intentions and reflect on the following.

- *What actions describe your good intentions? That is, what do you intend to do?*
- *Is there an earlier situation that has caused you to want to take action?*
- *Are you aware of any motives other than your best intentions—self-interest, guilt, shame, hidden hopes?*
- *Given those other motives or reasons, do you see any possibilities for misunderstanding?*
- *Are there any other possibilities for action that might better reflect the double-sided nature of this situation? What are they?*

The Dual-Sided Nature of Change

There is yet another complexity to consider. Taken at face value, the idea that good and evil coexist can be used inappropriately to rationalize any set of actions; any harm can be justified in the name of promoting positive change. *Yes, it's too bad we have to do X, but we need to do that in order to have Y.* In today's work environment especially, a high premium is placed upon change—sometimes for the sake of change itself and with little regard for its possible negative consequences. With the sweeping impact of such forces as globalization and the move to a digital economy, how important it is to consider the dual-sided nature of change. It is simply irresponsible to dismiss negative by-products with the claim that anything good requires sacrifice.

Cheryl's Story

TIMES HAD changed for my hometown of Herculaneum. We got incorporated, and getting a stop sign at the intersection of Main and the Old Highway was a big event. By the time I grew up, only the managers' houses belonged to the company, and automobiles enabled people to seek work in other towns nearby.

My father had become the plant manager. Friendly and well respected in the community for his concern for others, he walked through the hot, smelly lead-smelting plant every morning and greeted each employee. Yet I remember hearing his stern words as I was growing up, especially about employees that complained: "If they don't like it, they're free to leave. They should try to get a job somewhere else." Though I have a great deal of respect for my father, I don't know that he understood the implications of his words—that because exploitation is likely to be greater elsewhere, workers should be thankful for only a moderate degree of exploitation. No one used the word *exploitation,* of course.

My father's words sometimes haunt me, partly because I hear them so often today, but differently: "If we don't do it, someone else will." I hear these words as justification for destroying rain forests and marine life, for packing thousands of chickens into a truck for slaughter, for setting up cheap-labor manufacturing facilities overseas, and for contracting with sweat shops in the garment industry. The dilemma is that the words are often followed by "and if we don't do it, we will be out of business," which sometimes does, in fact, happen. Even at the plant in our town, I remember serious struggles for solvency in the face of increasing regulatory standards and periods of lower prices for lead.

The words "If we don't do it, someone else will" especially haunt me when I hear myself repeating them: "Everyone else does it, so why shouldn't I?" It is humbling to realize the thin line between our judgments and our self-justifications. ❧

In trying to reimagine the relationship of good and evil, we cannot escape the mocking of our own ideals. In the business world, there is great pressure to focus on the good—service, quality, efficiency, cost reduction. We have difficulty seeing how these things have unintended consequences and certain kinds of evil. Alternately, things that might normally foster self-interest and cynicism can be the source for something good. The challenge for us in examining the interplay of good and evil in work-based situations is to refrain from promoting an ideal as simply good or bad. Instead, recognizing that both are present, we can begin to consider how good and evil each give rise to the other. This has pragmatic value for situations that are polarized: We recognize that each perspective teaches us, that each offers a lesson that can inform us about appropriate actions.

Elie Wiesel, witness and survivor of the holocaust in Germany, tells a story about the battle of good and evil as he heard it from his grandfather. A long time ago, the soul of a great and pious man was to be sent down to Earth. Satan petitioned the celestial court, arguing that such a man would be so righteous and his teaching so persuasive that the choice between good and evil would become a moot point. "I will be beaten in advance. I demand justice," Satan argued. The celestial court agreed with his argument. The first soul would still be sent to Earth to inhabit a great Rebbe (teacher). But to reassure Satan, another soul would be sent to Earth with all the outward manifestations of piousness and righteousness, mirroring almost exactly the virtues of the first soul. What only Satan and the court would know is that this second soul's allegiance would be to Satan. "How is one to know? How does one recognize purity?" Wiesel asked his grandfather. And the grandfather told the young Wiesel, "But one is never sure; nor should one be."[3]

Finding that the wild-card other enriches us with new perspectives, we continue our exploration in the next chapter by cultivating a relationship with our shadow.

6

Shadow Sightings and Everyday Practice

The range of what we think and do
is limited by what we fail to notice.
And because we fail to notice
that we fail to notice
there is little we can do
to change
until we notice
how failing to notice
shapes our thoughts and deeds.[1]

—R. D. LAING

THERE IS MUCH IN everyday life, if we pause to notice, that points toward the shadow. While we've focused primarily on the hidden aspects of shadow, some are quite open and available for our viewing. Take, for example, the way we drive our cars on crowded, busy streets.

Rattling off a slew of obscenities in a moment of frustration from behind the wheel is not only permissible, but might even be seen as an indicator of strength. Although one does hear of these kinds of outbursts occasionally in the work environment, they are not generally acceptable. If someone's project is cut off by another project, the anger is usually played out more subtly, masked by a number of social conventions. But in the car, we let it rip. Other expressions of shadow acceptable in specific social circles include such things as fraternity hazing, the bachelor party, or excessive amounts of work being assigned to a younger associate.

Then there are vicarious forms of shadow expression. At football games, fans scream with delight as the favored team tramples the opponent, and the more brutal the blows, the better. Movies become a chance to live vicariously through screen characters who act out, on our behalf, our most fantastic ideals or our most feared behaviors. The blood and violence available on the screen these days provides ample opportunity for assuaging our darker nature. Pornographic films and materials, blood-letting sports such as boxing, movies and books about deception and betrayal, publicly televised criminal trials—all of these serve as outlets for vicariously gratifying the more aggressive instincts of our darker nature.

Are you aware of any particular tendencies of your own to express shadow that would fall into the category of socially acceptable or vicarious? What meaning do you ascribe to these tendencies?

Most expressions of shadow in everyday life are not so obvious, however, because of the very nature of shadow as the hiding place for what embarrasses us. It's uncomfortable. We'd rather avoid these things. While we may easily recognize the outbursts of someone else's dark side, only the trained observer can see within, to the manifestations of one's own personal shadow. The following table offers some hints for recognizing our own shadow dynamics in everyday life.

Everyday Shadow Indicators

Irreverence	When we cannot tolerate an irreverence for something, whether someone is poking fun at us or at something we value. This reflects a one-sided identity. Context is important here; there is also the case where teasing can go too far and irreverence is simply insensitive (also an indicator of shadow).
Humor	When we find something particularly funny. Whether a slapstick mishap, a body part, or someone's foibles, paying attention to what strikes us as funny can lead us to shadow awareness.
Covering up	When we don't want others to see something, when it's important to put a certain face forward, or when we feel humiliated or ashamed. Any desire to hide something or to create an impression that is misleading can be an indication of shadow.
Make-or-break situations	When we cannot afford to be seen as being a certain way, or when we must have a certain outcome (budget, contract, buy-in). Make-or-break situations seem to invite shadow activity, perhaps because of our vulnerability or one-sided dependence in the face of something so important.
Attachment to ideas	When we become so fond of an idea that we find it hard to tolerate those who point out its flaws. Perhaps we are polite but feel angry or put off for being questioned. Whether it applies to a perspective, a new love relationship, or a business strategy, the attachment seems to carry with it a certain blindness.
Us-them mentality	When group identity promotes a one-sided perspective of a situation. This happens often in a postmerger environment, or where there is tension between employees and management, when there are new owners of a business, or where extreme values or ideals have become boundaries for group identity.
Exaggerated feelings, judgments, or reactions	When we react strongly to others or judge them or when we are especially angry about others' faults. The exaggeration of feeling, whether positive or negative, is often an indication that something is being reflected from our inner world, perhaps in a distorted form, that we would rather only see "out there." (See *Application: Taking Back a Projection,* page 79).
Impulsive words or acts	When we spontaneously say or do things that reflect poor judgment. We may be surprised at our own words or actions and wish we could take them back. This can be an indication of underlying emotions that are uncomfortable and therefore stay hidden from us, such as anger with someone we care about.
Negative feedback	When we receive unexpected negative feedback from others, when we seem to have a troubling effect on others, or when we don't know what the feedback means or what to do with it. This is the "wild-card other," serving as a mirror. The shadow seems to use such feedback as a way to restore our balance, humbling us when we are overconfident, arrogant, self-focused, or inattentive. The confusion often centers around something we would prefer stay hidden.
Surprise attacks	In addition to receiving negative feedback, "surprise attacks" include finding that something we've done has backfired and that others have misunderstood or strongly disagreed with our actions, or finding ourselves negatively affected by a decision that is unexpected or seems unfair.

Referencing this last indicator, "surprise attacks," we might think of our personal shadow as something of a trickster—appearing suddenly and vanishing, laughing at us from behind our reflection in the mirror, or luring us down a path that seems reasonable, then disappearing just before the ambush. Whether felt as a sting or as a pleasant surprise, the trickster's revelations usually help us to restore balance, either humbling us in the face of an overinflated ego or upholding our nobility of character in the face of a deflated image of ourselves. Many everyday appearances of shadow, in fact, seem related to restoring our balance in the face of one-sidedness, beckoning us to hold in tension the opposites within ourselves. It seems that whenever we need to grow out of some aspect that keeps us stuck, the psyche does its work through the shadow, pushing us uncomfortably on toward wholeness.

When we suspect shadow dynamics may be at play, it helps to ask ourselves questions such as: *Is my reaction disproportionate to the circumstances? Why might this be happening to me now? What have I not been wanting to see? What belongs to me, and what belongs to others?* By asking the difficult questions and responding in ways that honor our reflections, we are owning our dark side, in essence taming its wildness and lessening the need for the shadow's eruptions.

That is not to say that shadow activity always starts and stops with the work we do on ourselves. We live and work with others and in systems that can take on a life of their own, so that we are sometimes subject to events over which we have no control. It's important to ask the questions that cut through to our own accountability—*How have I contributed to this dilemma? What are some actions I can take?* But this in no way should imply that we are totally accountable for difficult situations. Working with shadow material can be misused in that way, as if we are totally responsible for the system of which we are a part. Rather, the critical stance is to be willing to see *what piece* of the situation is ours. Understanding which piece is ours allows us to see which pieces don't belong to us as well. And this frees up our energy to be directed in more creative ways.

Reflection

RECOGNIZING OUR OWN SHADOW INDICATORS

Take a moment to consider the material of this section and the everyday indicators of your own shadow. In a relaxed setting, open to the possibility of the shadow working to restore balance to your life, and reflect on the following.

- WHICH OF the shadow indicators most attract your attention? Why?
- DO ANY indicate that you might need to grow out of something?
- ARE THERE situations in your near future that seem likely to invite shadow?
- WHAT ARE some ways that you can respond to these insights? Are there actions you can take to manage a particular situation differently, honoring its double-sided nature?

The Balancing Act

Loren was a happy-go-lucky attorney, never without a smile, a joke, a kind word. He seemed to have a close relationship with his spouse, children, and grandchildren. He was an excellent tennis player and worked out regularly in the gym. In short, by all outward appearances, Loren seemed full of life. One day as he left his house for his regular morning jog, Loren was met by the police. People at the tennis club were shocked to discover that he had been arrested and charged with insurance fraud. In fact, he was convicted and spent several years in jail for leading a multi-million dollar auto insurance fraud ring.

Loren's story happens every day—the television evangelist who is found to make regular trips to a prostitute, the role-model sports star who engages in criminally violent behavior, the non-profit administrator convicted of embezzlement. More often, we find the story played out in much subtler ways, in the tendencies of ordinary, successful people to sport such vices as white lies, multiple affairs, or cheating on taxes—and not just cheating on taxes, but especially loving to do so.

These situations are all indications of the darker side wanting its expression in light of the outwardly visible indicators of success, fame, or some form of goodness. When too much attention is placed (perhaps by others) on our good characteristics, the darker side of us rises up. Jungian analyst Robert Johnson described this phenomenon metaphorically as a seesaw: We have a socially acceptable side that we present to the outer world and another side, that does not seem acceptable, that we hide. All of our characteristics must be accounted for in this way, and—especially important—the seesaw must be balanced. Johnson writes:

> That is, the seesaw must be balanced if one is to remain in equilibrium. If one indulges characteristics on the right side, they must be balanced by an equal weight on the left side. The reverse is equally true. If this law is broken, then the seesaw flips and we lose our balance. This is how people flip into the opposite of their usual behavior. The alcoholic who suddenly becomes fanatical in his temperance, or the conservative who suddenly throws all caution to the wind, has made such a flip. He has only substituted one side of his seesaw for the other and made no lasting gain.[2]

The metaphor of the seesaw highlights the importance of maintaining equilibrium between our social persona and our private world. To the extent that we can consciously attend to our darker side—our lesser-known inner world—we are actively cultivating our relationship with the shadow and minimizing the likelihood of its disruptive bursts.

Up to this point in these chapters on shadow, most of the focus has been on *reacting* to the appearances of shadow. We shift the exploration, now, to a variety of ways to proactively seek out a healthy, constructive relationship with our dark side. In trying out some of these techniques for yourself, you may be surprised to find them enjoyable.

Cultivating a Relationship with Shadow

While the shadow remains ever-present, our relationship to it can change. We learn through our repeated encounters with shadow to be vulnerable to its sting, its comfort, and its humor. As with someone we've come to value and trust, over time we realize that the shadow can be a friend, a partner in making us whole. Moving beyond our reaction-based relationship with the shadow, the material in this section is geared toward *cultivating* a relationship with our shadow as a key to our wholeness.

How have you related to your darker nature in the past—with avoidance, impulsiveness, introspection, discomfort? How would you like to relate to this part of yourself going forward?

With the hustle and bustle of our lives, *cultivating a relationship with the shadow* is not something that would ordinarily fit into our routine. Given the house-of-mirrors nature of our inner life, we need separate space for allowing the balance to be sorted out. In this section, we'll suggest a variety of ideas for setting aside space for engaging with the darker aspects of our selves. Our hope is that you would be alert to your reactions as you read and take time to respond to the things that get your attention, crafting your own reflections and activities as you see appropriate. You might also make note of areas that you'd like to come back to at a later time.

SETTING ASIDE SPACE

Meeting the shadow calls for slowing the pace of life, listening to the body's cues, and allowing ourselves time to be alone in order to digest the cryptic messages from the hidden world.[3]

—CONNIE ZWEIG AND JEREMIAH ABRAMS

Space for Ritual

In the daily grind of the workplace, we are invariably confronted by darkness that is outside of ourselves. Customers are demanding, our work is stymied by political battles, meetings are filled with rhetoric or blame-ridden conflict. We can't help but get ourselves tangled up with things we think we shouldn't have said, things we wish we would have done differently, and difficulties we're not sure how to resolve. Though at times it may be so subtle and so ordinary that we hardly notice, the grit of the work environment takes its toll on us.

In a series of Navajo mysteries by Tony Hillerman, Officer Jim Chee must routinely deal with the darker aspects of human nature—fights break out, people are killing each other, or on a good day, there is lying, stealing, and double-crossing. Part of the allure of his character is his way of integrating his work life as a police officer with his spiritual practices. After each daily dose of the darkest aspects of human nature, Detective Chee invariably returns to the sweat lodge and gives himself over to the steam. Without his having to think through every dark moment, the ritual steam does its work on him, opening up his pores and dissolving the grime.

Through developing rituals, we can allow ourselves space to work out the exposure we've had to the darker side of life. This might be through conscious reflection, or it might be space in which we don't reflect on anything in particular, allowing the unconscious to do its own work through us. There are many other forms of ritual from which to choose:

- Walking in the woods or along water
- Meditation (including guided meditations, active imagination, or sitting)
- Prayer
- Sweat lodge (or a less "spiritual" version, the steam room)
- Journal writing

Any of these activities might be done spontaneously, in response to the corruption and dehumanization that we come into contact with in our work lives. It is important that we allow space, that we take time to be present and open, without trying to do anything in particular with it. Perhaps you have your own favorite activities that might be taken up as a kind of reflective (active or passive) ritual—driving in the mountains, sitting on a certain rock or under a certain tree, listening to a certain piece of music, gardening, cooking, weaving, or praying.

The activity itself is not as critical as the way in which we take it up—in order to digest the "cryptic messages from the hidden world." Cooking, for instance, would not work as a meditative ritual if other people are around and the clock is ticking. It might work if it is done with respectful quietness, if chopping vegetables is treated as a meditation, if time is taken to appreciate the colors, the textures, and the smells. Whichever activity you might choose to take up as a ritual, therefore, it is important to be mindful of quieting yourself and allowing your thoughts to settle into silence or to flow freely.

As a corporate attorney for a chemical conglomerate on the East Coast, Yvonne was assigned to Paris for several weeks, to manage the legal parameters of an acquisition. She quickly found the demands to be extraordinary in comparison with her more routine assignments. Not only were there conflicts related to the acquisition itself, but some of the legal issues were ambiguous in the new organization of the European Community, and the cross-cultural nuances were extremely tricky. Though quite competent in her work in the United States, she found herself struggling for the insight and the courage required of her in this situation.

Toward the end of her first week, Yvonne discovered a path from her hotel that led to the river. She followed the path along the river, walking amidst the quiet whispers of the leaves and the water. Though she didn't concentrate on anything in particular, she found this walk along the water to work on her like magic, restoring her general appreciation for life as well as her self-confidence.

Yvonne began returning to the river at the end of each day, even if she had only a small amount of time. On some days she simply couldn't, but she made this new activity a priority. She had found the walk to be an anchoring experience, and the water became a kind of friend for the difficult journey.

The ideal way to take up any kind of ritual is on a routine basis—daily, weekly, or for certain occasions annually. Regularity of ritual seems to allow it to work its way into us so that it requires less thinking about it—we just do it, because the sun is going down or because it's Wednesday evening. This is consistent with the notion of allowing space in which we do not have to think about things; rather, we simply allow ourselves to be with a situation and let the grime work its way through our system. Whether spontaneous or habitual, ritual represents a kind of Sabbath rest, a space in which we can step away and dissolve some of the contamination.

Space for Balance and Inquiry

The image of the seesaw suggests that we might do well to take time out to attend consciously to "the other side." Work places its demands on us, our personal lives make their demands, and we find ourselves struggling to remember why we decided to pursue this career or live in this neighborhood. How common it is to hear someone say, "I feel pulled into the current, swept downstream, and I feel very little choice in what I'm doing." Or, "I'm just going through the motions in this job, to finish out my last two years here." Such words indicate a loss of balance and the need for centering.

Sometimes our need for balance is not apparent to us, although we can see it in someone else—the need to chill out after some bad news, or to take a step down out of the halo. After a particularly outstanding success, for instance, how easy it is to get carried away with an inflated view of ourselves.

Alan's Story

SEVERAL MONTHS ago I had dinner with a colleague who was working day and night analyzing processes at an investment banking firm. Things were going well and she was justifiably proud of her efforts. We ordered wine with dinner and waited to toast her initial success.

For reasons we were to learn later—a new waiter and a change in how orders were processed—the wine didn't arrive. When the waiter passed our table, my colleague caught the waiter's attention with a look that could kill. I was surprised at what seemed an overreaction and some measure of entitlement, neither consistent with how I viewed my friend. I gave her a raised eyebrow and suggested that she was far too important a person to be kept waiting. Caught off guard by my teasing, she seemed at first miffed by my remark. And then she paused and smiled a bit painfully, "I am feeling impatient. Here I am, in downtown San Francisco, consulting at a premier investment banking firm and doing a damn good job. I guess I really do feel like a more superior human being." Laughing now a bit more easily, she acknowledged being a bit full of herself.

The waiter eventually returned, apologetic and with the wine in hand. We were able to assure him that our lives would go on, and he relaxed enough to tell us of the adjustments still needing to be smoothed out. My colleague was able to use the experience as an occasion to reflect and possibly to return to her work with a renewed sense of balance. ❧

Maintaining our equilibrium is something that is best done as ongoing *preventive maintenance*. The preventive maintenance function in a manufacturing environment is set up to systematically inspect various pieces of equipment and areas of the work environment. The principle is that replacing washers and pumps before they break will prevent uncontrolled breakdowns in the production process and, therefore, can save a plant millions of dollars annually. Likewise, conducting frequent inquiries into the other within is a way to keep the various parts of ourselves in optimal condition. This is not easy to do; the usual tendency is to look inside when a crisis hits or something is bothering us, but to otherwise pay little attention.

The following presents a menu of ideas for restoring balance or for general inquiry of our shadow.

• *Humble work*—After a notable success, balance the scorecard by taking up some sort of task that is humbling in its nature—cleaning toilets, scrubbing the garbage pails, digging in the garden, or doing some finger painting (yes, just like in kindergarten). Example: Jean is a weaver who lives communally with other artists and writers. One of their ways of dividing up monthly communal chores is by talking about who has been particularly successful that month, then offering that person the dirtiest and most humbling work. Jean finds it accomplishes two goals—members feel free to talk about their own and others' achievements, and the work itself tends to balance any inflationary pull.

• *Symbol of inspiration*—So far as our psyche is concerned, a symbol functions as a kind of container for the things causing anxiety or confusion, freeing us to focus our attention more constructively. When faced with a situation that challenges your sense of self-worth or self-confidence, light a candle or wear a piece of jewelry or carry an object that has meaning to you. Let it be a reminder for you of whatever you're trying to make conscious. Examples: Realizing how angry she can become with colleagues, Emily began lighting a candle while preparing to go to work, reminding her to balance her feelings with a focus on the task of the group. For strength and encouragement during a work reorganization, Steve carried a coin with a tiger on it, given to him as a child by his grandfather.

• *Journal writing*—While ritual journal recording of our thoughts and feelings is always good for centering, we refer to it here in a more specific context—to give room to a part of yourself that you've had to restrain. After being in a situation that has required significant restraint (for example, extended politeness or holding your tongue with customers or coworkers you find irritating), use your pen as a way to let your feelings and fantasies flow unrestrained in your journal. No rules, no self-criticism, no being nice, and no being good. An alternative use of journal writing is to write for a limited number of minutes in the voice of your internal critic. The Critic's voice can be painfully informative about our dark side, so use compassion when doing this. See chapter 3 for a review of giving voice to different aspects of ourselves in a constructive, contained way.

• *Art work*—In times of confusion or strong emotions, sometimes it is good to allow the unconscious space to do its work without an agenda. It's often surprising to see the richness of what gets expressed in free-form drawing or shaping clay. Perhaps there is an image in your mind, or perhaps not. Try allowing your hands to draw freely, using chalk, pencils, or paints to express whatever the psyche wants to express. Working with clay can be especially grounding, since it is, quite literally, from the ground and gives us a way to connect directly with the earth and its symbols of creation and death. If you work with clay, try allowing the clay to take whatever shape it wants to take. Whatever your mode of expression, it's important to let go of judgments about good and bad art; the term *soul work* may be more appropriate.

• *Dream work*—Dreams seem to be one of the primary ways the unconscious expresses itself. Consider keeping a notebook beside your bed and recording the dream within your first waking moments. If a particular dream image seems important to you, whether animate or inanimate, consider writing about it or dialoguing with it in your journal (yes, that's asking questions and imagining a response). Drawing the dream image is also a way to digest the cryptic messages about our inner other. If you normally don't remember your dreams, try recording even the vaguest of dream images or images that pass through your imagination; through such stimulation of your awareness, you should begin remembering more of your dreams. Review chapter 2 tips for working with fantasies or created stories, which is very similar to how we would work with dreams.

• *Describing the despicable*—Write a paragraph or two describing the characteristics of someone you find intolerable, whether someone you know personally or a character from a television show, a movie, or a book. Then treat what you have written as a direct projection, examining the ways in which it describes you directly or in a distorted form. Example: Late one evening, Marty finally decided to write down what bugged him about his manager. As the writing began to flow, the image of his boss began to take shape—a spineless mouthpiece for senior management who avoided conflict and kept putting decisions off. As Marty reflected on his portrayal, he could see more clearly how he and his boss were different from each other but also how his own avoidance of uncomfortable feelings had made it easier for him to put those feelings onto his manager. Marty shifted from blaming and moved more toward reflection about his own choices regarding conflict and uncomfortable situations.

• *Probing our attachments*—Another situation ideal for probing into the darkness, and quite common, is when we find ourselves having a strong attachment to certain ideas—a project proposal we intend to present, a promising business opportunity, or a conviction that someone needs to be fired. See *Reflection: Finding the Possibility of Evil* in chapter 5 on page 87. If you are unsure about whether there is a darker side to a situation, even if positive, consider experimenting. See *Strategic Questions for Our Best Intentions* in chapter 5, on page 90. Carl Jung wrote: "We can get lost in something which has strongly moved us, if we do not realize in time why we have become so affected by it. We should really once and for all ask ourselves the question: Why has this idea laid hold of me and affected me so much? What does it mean in relation to myself? This modest doubt can save us from becoming so entirely the victim of an idea of our own that we are swallowed by it for good and all."[4]

• *Soliciting feedback*—This can be a simple way to get more information about aspects of yourself that are difficult to see or accept. Feedback from others is a way to see through eyes other than your own. This could be particularly helpful if you are getting mixed messages about behavior that is bothersome to others or if you suspect others are not being direct in their responses to you. Here are some tips.

LET PEOPLE know why you are asking for their perspective—that you're concerned about the behavior and want to get a better understanding.

BE AS specific as possible about the behaviors in question—not just "How did I do?" but, "Am I allowing others enough opportunity to express their opinions?"

LET THEM know you want their input as a resource to consider along with others'. This lessens the weight on their shoulders to define your problems.

ASK FOR their honesty, and refrain from being defensive or argumentative about what they say. It's okay not to agree.

• *Getting into nature*—Placing ourselves in an environment where we can appreciate nature is an especially effective way to restore balance and cultivate inner wholeness. Through our contact with nature, we return to ourselves—to our own nature, perhaps. Example: Once or twice a year, Larry takes long walks in a state park not far from his home. Over the years, the walks have become a way to check in with himself and to ask himself if he still feels in charge of his life. For Larry, living deliberately is a crucial value and he finds that these walks remind him of his own nature. See the section "The Window of Metaphor" in chapter 2 on using nature as a way to see into our own inner wilderness.

This last point deserves special attention. There is something about nature that provides an opportunity to make contact with something outside of ourselves, something larger. As we appreciate nature, it is as if we take something of its beauty into ourselves. We are linking our inner world to what transcends us—to that which is ancient, powerful, organic. Art, poetry, or music can have this same impact.

By restoring beauty and balance, we are making space for shadow to be woven naturally into our lives. We come to work with new energy and new perspective, reaching toward a wholeness that is spiritual as well as personal.

The Lifelong Discipline

To honor and accept one's own shadow is a profound spiritual discipline. It is whole-making and thus holy and the most important experience of a lifetime.[5]

—ROBERT JOHNSON

Honoring and accepting our shadow means that we soften in our fears and open to its treasures. When we do this, we find ourselves tapping into some of the most spiritual aspects of our being. Here are some final reminders for the lifelong discipline of owning our own shadow.

ABOUT THE SHADOW

- The shadow is pervasive. *Basically, the shadow is present in every activity; we can never rid ourselves of shadow. Rather, it remains available to us as a rich source of learning for our movement toward wholeness.*

- Don't get stuck in the negative. *Every positive act has a potential for evil, and every negative act has a possibility for good. The shadow is present in both and should not be used to focus on the negative.*

- Don't use shadow as a way to make others wrong. *Be aware that it is easier to see someone else's darker nature than it is to see our own. The temptation to use our insights to prove our point or make others wrong can be enormous. While letting go of pieces in a situation that do not belong to us, we must use caution to resist the urge to assign blame or confront others prematurely.*

- Allow the awareness of shadow to be a source of creativity. *Whether caught by the shadow's surprise or engaged intentionally in shadow-seeking activity, it's helpful to remember the shadow as a storehouse for some of our most vital and creative aspects.*

- Enjoy the irreverence and humor that comes with shadow awareness. *As we begin to see more links between our inner frailties and things that are going on around us, we start to laugh at ourselves more. We see frailty, our own and others', as the imperfections that make us human.*

- Resist judgment when working with shadow. *Working with our hidden nature requires the ability to navigate across many different levels of meaning. It requires a part of us that can "see" without judging. If we're going to work with shadow, we must try to be compassionate and let go of judgments—toward ourselves as well as others.*

Working with our own shadow material enables us to respond more effectively to the many manifestations of shadow in organizational life. We learn to recognize the symptoms of shadow at work—how one-sidedness and projection can drain us of our energy and result in poor decisions or failed implementation of good ideas. We can deal with shadow strategically, by actively seeking out contingency plans, but more important, by allowing those with doubts to be valued and heard. Consideration of shadow allows us to see multiple representations of a problem, to see a concern from varied vantage points, and by doing this we find new links we had not seen before.

All of the work we do with shadow is a way of cultivating a relationship with the hidden aspects of ourselves. We learn about the health of our relationship to shadow by monitoring our responses to difficult situations. As we deal with the loss of a job, a complicated decision, or a personal difficulty such as divorce or death, what do we learn about ourselves in how we respond? Do we ignore the difficulty and busy ourselves with other things? Do we react in anger or with blame? Do we move toward quick resolutions that we know are not optimal? Or are we able to sit with the discomfort, allowing space for things to sort themselves out? As we practice sitting with what is uncomfortable, we develop the psychological muscle strength for holding something in tension, until it can be better understood, until something new can emerge.

You must carry the chaos within you in order
to give birth to the dancing star.

—NIETZSCHE

SECTION TWO

The Expedition

7

Finding Purpose
in Work

A PHILOSOPHY PROFESSOR announced a pop quiz consisting of
one essay question. He wrote the question on the board: "Why?"
The students wrote furiously for an hour and took their break. When
they returned, the professor opened with the news that no one had
passed the quiz. "The answer is, 'Why not?'" Students reacted with a
mixture of anger and curiosity, ranging from feeling tricked to "Of
course!" In the ensuing discussion, however, they wrestled with issues
of meaning and purpose in their lives. Why, for instance, do we get up
in the morning? Why not? Why were they there in class, studying?
What did they hope to do with their lives? Each question only led to
more questions, until the professor noted that the elusiveness of the
questions seemed to fuel the students' energy.

The question of purpose is not a trick question, yet it does drop us right into the question of "Why?" When purpose is clearly understood, our natural response is "Of course!"—just as we might respond upon hearing the professor's answer of "Why not?" Oh yes, it's simple, and we link our efforts with that sense of purpose without much further consternation. But when purpose is not clearly understood, finding it is somehow not so simple. In today's work environment, the search for purpose is further complicated by the chaotic pace of change, often leaving us in a state of perpetual disorientation.

In this chapter, we do not try to solve the riddle of purpose once and for all; on the contrary, we are likely to introduce more questions than answers. Our hope is to propose a framework for thinking about purpose and how it works in our lives. We examine purpose as a container for our hopes and longings, a link between ourselves and the world, a guiding star for our work lives, and a pact we negotiate along a journey. We will explore everyday issues that can cloud our sense of purpose and look at how purpose might be crafted. Similar to the mysteries of soul and shadow, which must be approached indirectly, purpose, too, has a mysterious, emergent quality. Finding purpose, therefore, has a lot to do with learning to tune our awareness to what is trying to emerge. In attending to the emergent, we discover the path that becomes our own unique journey.

As you begin this chapter, what understanding do you currently have of purpose in your work life? Do you think about it much? Do you long for it? Or do you have certainty about it?

A Container for Our Longings

The importance of purpose emerges most poignantly from the experience of loss and absence. Purpose links us to our lives, in the sense that it brings meaning and connection to what we do in the world. In that way, it links us to others as well, and the feeling of having a clear purpose often coincides with the feeling of belonging to a community that cares about what we do. But those linkages do not always seem solid in today's workplace. The impact of reengineering and job restructuring has left many of us with a workplace that feels empty. There is a profound sense of loss and absence—the absence of clear roles, the absence of our former colleagues and friends (or our boss), the absence of familiar surroundings, or the absence of a clear future.

Cheryl's Story

GROWING UP, I don't remember my parents or anyone else talking about purpose in work. It didn't seem to be a relevant issue. My father's loyalty to his company was a given, as was the company's loyalty to him. There was a sense of being a part of a company community. Roles were clear-cut, employment was for an entire career, and these things were not questioned. These former givens seem to linger today as false ideals, pulling on our longings for security and certainty. ✸

The experience of loss and absence may stem from other sources as well. Perhaps the ladder of success has taken you to a place absent of your values. You never intended that to happen, yet here you are. Or perhaps, slowly, you have lost sight of the reason you decided to go into your field in the first place. It's not what you expected, the paperwork is overwhelming, the obstacles are draining. Or perhaps there is loss in your life due to the cost of your efforts. Has your work life cost you a sense of wholeness in your family life? Has it cost your connection to your inner world or to nature? Has it cost your health?

The feelings of emptiness sometimes call out to us, awakening us from our slumber and agitating us until we find ourselves on a search. Not knowing quite what it is we need, we long for something greater, something real, something that can survive the onslaught of the daily grind and bring satisfaction to our lives. Purpose offers us the possibility of satisfaction—not simply success and happiness, but a deeper sense that what we strive for is worthy of our efforts.

*As you think about the rhythm of your work life and the costs of
your efforts, what do you find missing?*

Purpose also contains longings that are tied to our hopes and
dreams. We long to express our creativity, to make a difference, to
be appreciated. Or we long to feel again the urgency of something
worth doing, or to know what it is we really want in our lives.

Our hopes represent the deepest, most important parts of
ourselves. Imbedded with our values, they offer the key toward
purposeful living. With hopes clearly in mind, we have added
stamina for the tasks and obstacles we face. A sense of purpose
helps us to carry our hopes toward fulfillment and face obstacles without giving up. Early in his career, for example, Willie
Nelson could not get airtime on the radio, because his music
was deemed neither country nor blues. Unwilling to let these
obstacles stand in his way, Willie kept playing.

Sometimes our hope is inspired by earlier dreams that connect us with purpose or encourage us along the way. What made
us feel most alive? What gifts and talents were revealed? When
did we want to be noticed? There are moments in our lives
when having a dream, regardless of its viability, can inspire us to
press on.

Alan's Story

WHEN I was eleven or twelve, I was convinced I would play
professional baseball. I was fast around the bases, had
good range in the field, and could punch the ball into right field.
My hero was Yankee second baseman Bobby Richardson. He
caught the last out in the 1962 World Series, a hard line drive
from Willie McCovey. When I heard the crack off McCovey's bat,
I think my heart stopped.

In high school, when I did not make the baseball team, I had
to accept that my dream of professional ball was never going to
happen. The realization of limitation, however, was not my only
lesson. The fantasies that accompanied my longing to play ball

taught me that it was okay to dream, that there was joy in imagining myself rounding first base on my way to second, hitting a rocket down the line, and catching the last out in a championship series. At times, in my adult life, when the mundane threatens to take over, I can feel distanced from even having any dreams. But in my heart, when I am honest with myself, I still hear the crack of the bat and the crowd rising up as one. The game is on the line. And I am so alive. ❧

Perhaps because hope is so potent, it has inherent complexities that we simply need to be aware of: First, we are vulnerable to idealizing what we want. Idealizing pulls us into one-sidedness and invites our shadow to surface, clouding our hopes with the darker aspects of our nature. Bruce, for example, had hopes of becoming partner in his New York law firm. Seeing this as a way to distinguish his career and multiply his income, he had decided to "go for it."

These hopes led him to make enormous sacrifices in his personal life and professional values, until he reached a point of exhaustion and disenchantment. He understood, finally, that these sacrifices would continue, even as partner, and that he'd idealized what partnership meant: Instead of having more control of his life, there were more demands on it. Instead of having enough money, there was always a need for more. Instead of feeling powerful, he felt imprisoned. With reflection about what truly matters to him, Bruce is now considering other professional options that are less glamorous but offer more balanced fulfillment.

Another complexity is that fear goes hand in hand with the possibility of hope. Hope taps into some of the deepest parts of ourselves, and our fears get activated. The parts of ourselves that are fearful may fight to keep our hopes at bay: *What if I don't reach my hopes? What if I'm left with only the knowledge of what I truly long for? Better to not know at all and not have the pain.* Or, *It would have meant too much rehearsal time anyway.* Purpose challenges us to move with and through our fears, to open to our deepest desires, and to own those fears and desires as our own.

We must remember to listen as well to the inner voice that says, *I really want to do this. I can do it, it's possible.* And we must be prepared to pursue what is real and possible.

Linda always wanted to be a movie producer but felt trapped in her day job of producing television commercials. In the industry, producing commercials carried a stigma that she felt hindered her access into film. Having worked hard just to get where she was, she discounted her dream as a lofty ambition, not realistic. One day a friend got tired of hearing her complain and challenged her about her attitude. A bit taken aback at first, Linda finally came to terms with the fact that her dream of producing a movie was realistic. It was only her fear and lack of appropriate action that held her back. With a sense of purpose, a plan of action, and the discipline of follow-through, Linda devoted her energies more fully to producing a movie. Two years later, a major cable network aired her first film.

Whether haunted by our longings or inspired by our hopes, a sense of purpose allows us to be more integrated in how we approach our work. Daunting as well as life-affirming, the good news about purpose is that, for all of us, there is something of significance for us to do; the bad news is that we have to find out what it is and do it. It takes a fair amount of courage and inner strength to hold these conflicting parts of ourselves in tension, not only to find our purpose in work, but to pursue it as well.

 ## Reflection

CHECKING IN

- WHAT IS it that you truly long for in your work?

- WHAT KEEPS you from it?

- HOW DO the voices of fear speak to you?
  What do they say?

- IF YOU could imagine the voices of fear taking a sabbatical, what might you do?

On Being and Becoming

Flow with whatever may happen and let your mind
be free. Stay centered by accepting whatever you are doing.
This is the ultimate.[1]

—CHUANG TZU

Do not follow where the path may lead. . . . Go instead
where there is no path and leave a trail.

—ANONYMOUS

Each of these quotes inspires our way of approaching life, but in very different ways. The first is about the nature of *being:* Be still. Cultivate inner peace. Be present. Be happy in whatever circumstance you're in. The second is about the nature of *becoming:* Be all you can be. Go for it! Do whatever it takes. Blaze a new trail! Both offer valuable lessons, and both have extremities that can impair us. These approaches link our inner life to the outside world and help us to orient ourselves in the search for purpose at work.

Being is essential to purpose, because it awakens in us the instinct for what is most true in ourselves and links us to the deeper meaning behind our day-to-day actions: At work, *being* teaches us to be fully present in whatever we do. Rather than rushing between meetings or talking on the phone while we have one eye on our e-mail, we learn to appreciate the space between things. We consciously allow our attention to shift, from the conflict we've just left to what is important in the meeting ahead of us. We all know how wonderful it is to be with someone who gives us their full attention, as if nothing else in the world matters to them. This quality of being begins from a tiny seed of spaciousness within and is expressed by our being present and available to others. This not only helps us to use our time more effectively, but it also *frees* us to attend to the more subtle matters that are critical but that often go ignored. *Being* creates the space for attending to our values, to what matters, to the words we would choose and the actions we would take, as well as to the often subtle and unspoken values, fears, hopes, and concerns of others.

Becoming is essential to purpose, because it stops us from succumbing to the paralysis of fear: At work, *becoming* teaches us to appreciate the potentiality emergent in ourselves and others. Rather than simply protesting a change initiative or complaining about the idiocies of the work environment, we learn to take personal responsibility for making things better. We consciously try to sense into what might be possible, alert to feelings as well as thoughts. We all know how refreshing it is when someone can roll with the punches and deal with problems in a constructive way. What a relief to not just wallow in "how things are." An orientation toward becoming frees us—to change, to pursue new goals, to develop new disciplines, to experiment with new tactics, to grow into a new role, as well as to see the possibility in a new program, a new supervisor, or a new organizational structure.

Being and *becoming,* because they offer unique perspectives, can sometimes seem to pull at us in contradictory ways. *Being* implies stillness, *becoming* implies motion. *Being* respects the passive, *becoming* respects the active. *Being* suggests a satisfaction with the fullness of the moment, *becoming* suggests a dissatisfaction that presses us forward. We all know the maxim, "Don't just stand there, do something!" A recent counter maxim speaks to the side of *being*: "Don't just do something, stand there."

While we may recognize the value both bring, we remain vulnerable to their darker sides. The shadow of *being* is laziness, complacency, abandonment of responsibility, and self-absorption. The shadow of *becoming* is either that we shift into autopilot, going through the motions without thinking about their significance, or that we abuse ourselves by pushing the envelope.

Being and *becoming* counterpoint each other, therefore, challenging us to hold them in tension and reminding us to bring balance to what has been neglected. Through cultivating awareness of our true nature and taking personal responsibility for our actions, purpose becomes linked with the idea that what we do matters. In that sense, purpose becomes one of those places where our spiritual lives and our work lives can join.

In your work life, how are you pulled by being and becoming? In what ways might you bring them into better balance?

By offering this link between our spiritual and work lives, purpose provides a framework for meaning. It reminds us that *how we bring ourselves,* in whatever we do, is a mirror to our soul. There is the story of three stonemasons and a visitor to the city who asked each what he was doing. The first one said, "I'm cutting stones." The second one said, "I'm making a wall." And the third one said, "I'm building a cathedral."

By linking us to the world and to meaning, purpose also links us to the transcendent. By transcendence, we mean the experience of being a part of something larger, serving a greater good, and the internal experience of awe. We touch the transcendent when we witness beauty, grace, or magnificence, or when we feel ourselves as a participant in what we witness— standing at the precipice of the Grand Canyon, walking beneath a full moon, feeling the spray of a waterfall. We touch the transcendent when we witness extraordinary acts of human effort and accomplishment—Mother Teresa's ministry to the socially outcast, Michael Jordan's performance on the court, Cirque du Soleil's mastery of the body. We touch the transcendent when we identify with an organization that has a purpose greater than our own—the Marines, Greenpeace, or an Internet start-up. Transcendence also weaves itself into day-to-day human endeavors such as our neighbor's tutoring of underprivileged children on Tuesday afternoons, or a manager's insistence that people go home at the end of the workday, or the janitor's warm smile that reveals an inner dignity.

The question is not so much how work can be transcendent, but *how we allow the transcendent to enter our work.* Is it by reaching for the extraordinary? Is it by appreciating the simple? Is it by bringing dignity into the mundane? The answer is very personal, because of the way transcendence touches into our spiritual selves.

How *do* we allow the transcendent to enter our work? Sometimes it is through a willingness to be more of our true selves—to find expression for what we really care about.

Alan's Story

A COLLEAGUE TOLD me about talking with an old college friend, now an anesthesiologist in New York. The friend was doubting that career choice, feeling anesthesiology was so highly technical that it was beginning to feel mechanical. She found the experience with surgeons alienating as she listened to their banter during operations about the previous day's football scores. "But you manage the healing environment," my friend reminded her. "You're at the boundary between the patient and the surgeons." My friend's comment startled the anesthesiologist because she never thought about her work this way. And as the question echoed inside her, she began to see how she might act differently. She asked a patient, a man recently relocated from India and preparing for surgery, if there was any music he particularly loved and would want played during his surgery. The man was somewhat incredulous. Why would it matter if he was asleep? But he finally agreed and brought in a CD of sitar music that he particularly liked.

During the surgery, the music played, and the doctors performing the surgery were curious about what it was. She told them it was sitar music and explained it was the patient's choice. The music had the effect of creating a very different atmosphere within the surgical theater, with less banter or cynical comments and a tone something like reverence that pervaded the space. When the patient came out of surgery and unconsciousness, his recovery went remarkably smoothly. And for the anesthesiologist, the experience reconnected her with a larger purpose that was at the same time an expression of what she truly cared about. ✤

Reflection
ALLOWING FOR THE TRANSCENDENT

- WHAT EXPERIENCE with nature has inspired you with its beauty or grandeur? What do you remember thinking? feeling?

- WHAT HUMAN actions have inspired you, on a large scale or on a smaller one?

- IN WHAT ways do you recognize the transcendent in your own true nature, within your own *being*—perhaps an element of grace and beauty, or an awareness of divine presence, or the feeling of being a part of something larger, or a desire to serve a greater good?

- IN WHAT ways have you given expression to this aspect of your self or withheld it?

- AS AN expression of the potentiality within you, the part of you that is *becoming,* how might you allow more of this transcendence into your work?

Purpose in work takes on a transcendent nature when we link inwardly, with what is most true and natural for ourselves, and outwardly, with something of importance larger than ourselves. An awareness of *being* and *becoming* alerts us to the transcendent in purposeful work, whether saving lives or laying bricks. In opening to the transcendent, purpose might lead us to a different path than the one we're currently traveling, requiring major changes in our work. Alternatively, in opening to the transcendent, purpose might deepen our appreciation for the path we're on, inviting us to engage more fully and creatively in our existing work. Or the sense of purpose we discover might represent some hybrid of paths, work that takes a new turn or that joins us with an earlier path. Learning to listen to our inner voice, we learn also to trust the messy and often sideways process that leads us to where we are going.

A Guiding Star for the Journey

In the story of the three wise men who traveled from afar to bring gifts to the baby Jesus, it was a star, shining brightly, that guided their journey. We might think of purpose as a kind of guiding star for our work lives. We may travel south to avoid a mountain range or north to go around a body of water, but in the quiet of the night, we allow the star to direct and redirect our orientation.

In the story, the star was a kind of miracle, its unusual brilliance arousing the curiosity of the wise men and inspiring them. In our work lives, it is no different. When we see how our work is transcendent, even in a simple way, our journey becomes connected with "something more" at multiple levels—the unique gifts we have to offer, the meaning we associate with our day job, the linking of our journey with the journeys of others, and a general sense of destiny that eases the discomforts of the travel.

One of the most striking benefits of finding purpose in work is clarity of mind. We no longer need to flounder around half-heartedly with unclear aims; rather, we can make decisions and take actions based on their overall relation to purpose: Might a decision move us *toward* our sense of purpose in the long run, or *away* from it? This clarity is only possible when we are willing to confront our fears and open to our deepest longings. Otherwise purpose may seem lost, hidden within the clouds of doubt and dread. Though we may struggle with doubt and dread periodically throughout the course of our work lives, a sense of purpose provides a way for us to move through *that* wilderness.

Cheryl's Story

SOMETIMES WE are led into the struggle of finding purpose by a discontent with current circumstances, as in the anesthesiologist story above, and as in my own situation several years ago. Not knowing specifically how I wanted to refocus, I knew only that work was increasingly depleting my energy, creativity, and skills. Unlike the anesthesiologist, I could not find a way to reverse that in the situation I was in and decided to leave.

The options for next steps were numerous and divergent enough that, without a clear sense of purpose in my career, I would likely flounder. Knowing that I needed to be more anchored by a sense of purpose, I began to reflect on what I most valued about work and life. Trying to set aside fears about how I might go forward, my longings began to emerge, until I was able to develop something like a vision statement for my career: "to be a conduit of openness and growth, for those who are receptive, by bringing focus to their deepest desires, understanding of themselves in role, and illumination of pathways for the journey."

An advantage of this kind of vision is that it is open-ended enough to allow for flexibility. The good news and bad news is that it does not resolve every dilemma. Nevertheless, it is the anchor I've needed—a kind of yardstick for measuring whether a decision might move me toward my sense of purpose or away from it. It may shift over time, but for now this sense of purpose seems to provide helpful guidance for writing, consulting, net-working, and other work-related efforts. ❧

Whether we find our work to be purposeful is a deeply personal matter. Whether corporate, small business, or public service, the form and structure are not as important as the passions that purposeful work taps into. And for purpose to be sustaining, it needs to be linked with something outside ourselves, something transcendent.

What is worthy of your efforts? What evokes your gifts? What brings out the best in you? What is the greater good that you're serving?

WARNING!
"PURPOSE NOT PROVIDED HERE"

Many organizations, for multiple reasons, are not places where finding or acting with purpose is encouraged. There is a humorous story about the director Alfred Hitchcock, who was once asked by an actor for the motivation of his character in the

scene. Hitchcock told him, "Your salary." Unfortunately, this atti-
tude can create a real horror in the workplace, for those whose
roles leave little room for creativity, flexibility, or involvement—
especially when the salary is hardly at a subsistence level. For
2000, the U.S. Labor Department estimates that among the
largest growth in jobs will be cashiers, janitorial services, retail
clerks, and restaurant positions. For many in these roles, work
can be numbingly routine, and the question of purpose can seem
impossibly distant. Any position, adequately compensated or not,
can be a drag on the human spirit if purpose is not attended to.

As members of organizations and as citizens of society, we
would do well to try to create work that is meaningful, including
compensation that allows for a living wage. And as individuals,
we need to know that purpose is central to our well-being, and
that we cannot expect an organization to hand it to us preformed.
We each must construct it out of the clay of our own lives.

Just as the nature of purposeful work is personal, so is the
journey finding it. The search often requires us to wrestle with
the deeper questions—questions that stir up trouble. Realizing
how shallow our focus may have been, for example, we may feel
empty; or realizing how daunting a more meaningful pursuit
might be, we may feel overwhelmed. The issues pull at our passion and expose our hardwiring. As we rise to challenges worthy
of our efforts, we must at the same time be able to make peace
with the mundane. Filled with paradox and probing into the
deepest parts of ourselves, the journey toward purpose brings
our spirituality into relationship with our work lives and vice
versa. It is, therefore, always a personal journey, unique to our
own wilderness.

Sometimes we are pulled into the journey by unsettling circumstances. Julia is a plastic surgeon who found herself increasingly isolated from her professional colleagues. The predominant
focus in her field is on cosmetic surgery for the wealthy, for

which insurance companies are largely irrelevant. Julia's preference to perform corrective surgery (largely stemming from serious accidents or deformities) meant daily battles with insurance companies to collect fees and, in some cases, simply waiving fees for those with little or no income. Though successful in her specialty, Julia felt herself struggling to maintain her practice in a way that her colleagues serving the rich seemed to avoid. In addition, presentations at professional conferences seemed to shift increasingly toward the nuances of "beauty," causing her to feel even less connected to her field.

Ironically, a personal relationship led Julia to the decision to relocate and set up a new practice in Los Angeles—home of Tinsel Town and the plastic surgery capital of the world. Regardless of her specific focus, Julia knew that she could be successful in L.A. In addition to her competence and her easy way with people, being one of the few female surgeons in her profession would open a lot of doors. Indeed, several other surgeons began making offers, while encouraging her to pursue corrective work.

Predictably, the obsession with outward appearance so prevalent in L.A. agitated Julia. She became increasingly conflicted about her work. Finally, in turmoil, she decided to postpone all decisions and take some extended time off to think about what was important.

Julia became inspired with the potential of the Internet for delivering the latest in medical information to those in remote areas. In her conversations, she found herself talking about a worldwide collaboration of physician specialists who would post standard diagnoses and treatments on the Web. Soon she began to gather these treatment inputs, arrange them into Web-size pages, then post them online, one treatment at a time. Because of her efforts, physicians in the remotest of locations now have access to the latest in knowledge and procedures.

Julia's journey did not stop with the Internet. To explore some of the needs in less-developed countries, she arranged a six-week trip through Africa. During this time, she found herself performing emergency and corrective plastic surgery at every location, as well as training local doctors in specific surgical techniques.

Fatigue set in, as she found there was always more to do. Yet she felt the renewal of love for her work energizing her.

Julia is back in Los Angeles but still very much on a journey. She doesn't know exactly how she will move forward, but her sense of purpose in her work is clearer each day. A couple of days a week, to pay the bills, she performs outpatient surgery at a nonprofit clinic for anyone who walks in, on a sliding-fee basis. On other days, she networks with surgeons to contribute expertise or finances to the Internet project. With a lot of obstacles and the awareness of a much greater need than she can possibly address, Julia's day-to-day inspiration lies in greater clarity about who she is and what she most cares about.

Sometimes we stumble accidentally onto a sense of purpose. Paul is also a surgeon, but his journey did not begin with any specific sense of purpose at all. In fact, he saw his entry into the medical field not as a choice, but rather as a dutiful response to his physician father's wishes. In the course of pre-med classes, in which he felt quite detached, he became sick and was admitted overnight at the nearby hospital. During the night the man he shared the hospital room with grew worse, moaning and vomiting blood. Doctors and nurses flooded into the room, and the chaos and commotion became frantic. In the midst of the wrenching sounds and putrid smells, Paul found himself thinking, "I can't wait to be doing this!"

Sometimes the journey gets very pragmatic. In the story earlier in the chapter, Linda's dream of producing a movie became a reality only after she allowed it to guide her day-to-day work. Owning her hopes and fears rather than being held captive by them, she found a way to move systematically through those fears and toward her hopes. She listed all of her fears and any real or imagined obstacles, looking for what was underneath them: *I can't produce a movie because I'm not part of a production group, and I'm not part of a production group because I don't have the network I need, and I don't have a network because I'm too afraid to reach out, and I'm afraid to reach out because I don't want to show I need help. . . .* She then devised a plan, with specific goals and time frames, to develop the network and skills that would move her one step at a time toward her dream of producing a movie. She also enrolled a colleague to be her coach—to meet or speak with her daily and "hold her accountable" for progress against those goals, no excuses.

That was the easy part. More difficult was the daily grind of following through with her plan. If Linda slipped in reaching a goal, which she often did, her coach would grill her about her actions, her commitment, her revised goal, and her need for support to reach that goal. Some parts of the plan she did not care for at all, such as making five calls a day to expand her network. Yet she learned to see her dislike for such tasks in relation to her ultimate aim: *Am I going to forfeit my dream,* she would ask herself, *because I don't feel like calling Peter Pumpkin-Eater this morning?* Linda learned the importance of "holding the goal sacred," referring to the ultimate goal of producing a movie as well as each interim goal along the way.

"Holding the goal sacred," in fact, gave Linda the strength to undertake the most disliked and mundane tasks. She understood that in picking up the phone and risking disappointment, time and time again, she was producing her movie. Regardless of the outcomes of any specific actions, she learned to celebrate the accomplishment of holding steady to the plan and reaching small goals. As her ability to concentrate increased, the distractions decreased and opportunities emerged. Linda's sense of purpose became a mantra that played in the background of every activity.

What's the nature of your journey? When has it been moved along by uncomfortable circumstances? When have you stumbled into purpose? When have you been most pragmatic about it?

A sense of purpose in our work requires that we attend to both the inspiring and the pragmatic; otherwise inspiration remains lofty and purpose unfulfilled. As a guide for our work lives, purpose intersects several building blocks of success—the overarching vision or purpose itself, goals that help move us in that direction, a specific plan of action, skills to maneuver across obstacles, and the willingness to "hold the goal sacred." In addition, sharing our vision with others and enlisting their support can dramatically increase the likelihood of our success.

Reflection

BUILDING YOUR DREAM

In a relaxed setting, take time to reflect on your deepest hopes about your work. Imagine what your "cathedral" looks like, then drop down to the level of the cathedral walls, of bricks, and of the tools you will need.

- WITH REGARD to your hopes and dreams about work, what inspiration awakens you? Is it specific, or is it general?

- WHAT SCARES you about it? What excites you?

- WHAT NEEDS to happen along the way in order for you to reach this vision of your work?

- WHAT KIND of support do you need from others?

- WHAT ONE or two things can you do now, to move toward your vision?

Sometimes the journey is not necessarily about purpose. Often in the absence of purpose, we lack general feelings of fulfillment as well. Though not surprising, this can be tricky. Feelings of fulfillment often have a great deal to do with working effectively, as well as with our needs for community, belonging, and appreciation. In such cases, finding purpose may not be so lofty an endeavor; rather, it may be a matter of restoring balance, with work habits that increase our effectiveness.

CHECKLIST FOR EFFECTIVE WORK

- *Have you developed good communication skills, especially deep listening? (In deep listening, the focus is on relationships and inquiry—seeking information but not judging, being willing to consider the dual nature of issues.)*

- *Do you cultivate awareness as a work practice, such as focusing on the task at hand?*

- *Do you plan your work? If so, are your plans realistic, and do you follow them up with your actions?*

- *Do you pause to appreciate your accomplishments?*

- *Are you clear about your role (the focus of our next chapter)?*

- *Do you need to improve in any technical skills?*

- *Are you managing your energy, or does overwork and fatigue lead you to waste time?*

- *How do you bring yourself at work? Do you engage fully in what you do, or are you caught in halfheartedness? Do you look for creative ways to express your uniqueness or your spirituality in your work?*

- *Are your efforts aligned with the needs of the organization? In other words, are you doing the right things?*

- *Do you take your work too seriously? (This is related to the principle of one-sidedness, which causes us to lose balance.) Can you laugh at yourself? Do you need to let go of things you can't control?*

Even when it seems we have utter clarity in our work, we can never rest assured that we have found our life's purpose once and for all. A fixed and unchanging purpose can be a distraction from the more important questions and can dull our energy and creativity. On the contrary, purpose is elusive and needs to be. It keeps us slightly on edge, so that we are never completely sure, and it helps us to calibrate. It forces us to be open to the unexpected, to reexamine our views, to watch after what we most value.

Application
ALLOWING PURPOSE TO EMERGE

Purpose in work crosses over many different layers of our lives— from how we think about ourselves in general to the meeting we have this afternoon. In this application, you'll have an opportunity to reflect on a variety of questions relevant to finding purpose in work and, if you choose, to write something that could function as your own personal statement of purpose.

In your journal, write quickly whatever comes to mind:

1. WHAT IS it that you feel most passionate about?

2. WHAT ARE some of the things you most enjoy doing or would like to learn (*for example, a new software program, yoga, photography*)?

3. WHAT ABOUT your current work do you most enjoy? What would you like to do more of?

4. WHAT ABOUT your current work do you least enjoy? What would you like to do less of?

5. IF YOU weren't a (your major occupation), what would you be? Why?

6. WHAT DO you like or dislike about where you live?

7. WHAT KIND of civic or neighborhood involvement is important to you?

8. IMAGINE THAT you are looking back over the life of your career. What would you like to be known for?

9. HOW DO you think about money? What meaning or importance does it have for you?

10. HOW DO you think about family? What *is* "family" to you, and what meaning does it hold?

11. HOW DOES soul or spirituality show up for you at work?

12. WHAT DOES work mean for you? Is it a career, a statement of who you are, just a job or a paycheck, a social outlet?

13. WHAT IMPORTANCE do you give to your physical fitness and health?

14. WHAT, IN terms of people, seems most important to you in your work?

15. WHAT ELSE comes to mind?

A view from multiple angles:

- CONSIDER YOUR reactions in reading this chapter, the reflections, and perhaps your answers to these questions. What struck a chord for you emotionally? What longings have emerged?

- CONSIDER REVIEWING your answers to questions 1 through 15 from the perspective of shadow. For example, if you responded that money is not important to you, is there a shadow such as fear of what money might do to you or of your ability to earn what you want? What insights come to mind, as you contemplate the other side to your responses?

- CONSIDER YOUR responses to all of these questions (1 through 15, as well as those just above). What themes or patterns emerge? Write four or five sentences in your journal that express these themes.

Putting it together:

- NOW STEP back, perhaps with a cup of tea or by taking a walk. Allow the patterns and responses to roll over in your mind and in your heart. Does there seem to be coherence, to the extent that you can identify or describe a sense of purpose in your work? When you're ready, write this in a sentence or paragraph in your journal as if talking to a friend.

If you wrote a statement just now, consider taking a moment to appreciate your work. If you didn't write a statement, consider taking a moment to simply sit with *that,* acknowledging your insights, your ambivalence, your varied reactions. In either case, be attentive to your thoughts as they continue to emerge.

However we might express a sense of purpose in our work, it's important that we hold it gently, protectively, and loosely—as a gift to be thankful for. While our deepest values are not likely to change a great deal, our sense of purpose may shift as we grow and develop. Some flexibility is helpful, therefore. Clarity is wonderful and important; then letting go of the clarity is important, too, so that we might be jostled out of our comfort zones and into the next phase of awareness and growth.

Some people prefer to review the direction of their lives on a periodic basis, such as a birthday or the new year. A ritual like going into the mountains alone or writing reflections in a journal can aid us in periodically taking a fresh view of our sense of purpose in work.

What tradition do you have, or would you like to have, for thinking about purpose in your life and work?

We might think of holding our sense of purpose as an *intention* that we use to check against the direction of our decisions. How would purpose inform you, for instance, about whether to relocate for that new opportunity? or to risk raising concerns in the meeting this afternoon? or to go out of town on your child's birthday? or to let go of how you think something should happen?

A sense of purpose can guide us as a shining star in the quiet of the night, by which we course-correct our lives; or it can be a yardstick, by which we measure our day-to-day decisions and activities. It is not that we will never stray from our sense of purpose. The question is, can we hold onto purpose as an intention, so that our general movement is *toward* fulfillment and deepening? And when we stray, can we return again to ourselves?

8

Role As an Expression of Soul

Something we were withholding made us weak,
Until we found it was ourselves.

—ROBERT FROST

T HE NEATLY CARVED-OUT roles of the modern era have disap-
peared. Traditional hierarchical relationships are confounded by
matrix, team-based, and even virtual organization designs. Gone are
the cut-and-dry performance reviews, clearly written job descriptions,
and even private office space. Mergers, spin-offs, and frequent restructuring mean constantly shifting positions and roles. Reporting relationships are less direct, often remote, and performance management
systems are increasingly complex. Job descriptions can't capture all of
what we do, ongoing responsibilities compete with project-based initiatives, and process changes require constant adaptation to the work

itself. Not only are we confused about our own roles, but the shifting roles of our colleagues leave us unsure of where to go for support and collaboration. It's no wonder that, in the attempt to hold on to our sanity, we learn to withhold parts of ourselves. And then *that* weakens us, because we are split, and parts of ourselves are not present.

In this chapter, we explore role as an expression of who we are in relation to ourselves, to others, and to our work. Role is not simply an established position with clear responsibilities; rather, it involves both the position and the person: What is most true about ourselves? What are the most real and tangible aspects of the work? How can we make sense of our environment, so our actions can have relevance? What really matters? Role links this interior life of thought and emotion with the needs of an organization, awakening in us the creative tensions, polarities, and even contradictions.

What Is Role?

As authors who link role with soul, we thought it might be useful to provide some conceptual anchors and images.

• Role is the coming together of the person and the position, so that the strengths of both are brought to bear on the work of the organization. Role invites us to translate the anonymous elements of any job and stamp it with our own personality. When we work to construct a role for ourselves, therefore, we are participating in a creative act, something that has never been done before. This takes great courage, discipline, and an appreciation for being part of something larger than ourselves.

• We express who we are through our various roles. The intensity of our personality, the seriousness of our purpose, the ambivalence of our feelings—all of these take on meaning within the context of a role. Rather than trying to eliminate the personal and idiosyncratic dimensions of the person, role includes what is true and natural about ourselves—a critical source for the creativity and innovation that organizations so badly need.

- Bringing one's whole person into the work imbues the work with purpose and meaning. Regarding ourselves and others as being worthy of dignity precedes and encompasses doing work that is important. Ironically, sometimes it is by participation in meaningful work that we discover the worth of each individual.

- Role requires a mental and emotional alertness to the "system" we are in. For this reason, we need to show up and be present to what is unfolding in the here and now.

- Analogous to soul and purpose, role acts like a container that can hold multiple tensions, polarities, paradox, and even irreconcilable differences that exist within individuals and groups. The person, embodying human need, and the organization, embodying group need, create a dynamic friction and complexity that is greater than the sum of its parts. The stronger the sense we have of our role, the more *heat* we can take and the greater capacity we have to be creative with the complexity.

- Role acts as a joint does in the human body, joining two elements and allowing flexibility and motion. Person and position is one example of how role unites two separate ideas. Similarly, reflection and action are linked in role. Having the right idea about what to do is of limited value if not acted upon, and acting without understanding the causes and consequences of our actions is equally problematic.

THE ORGANIZATION AS A WHOLE

Role implies that we are part of something larger. We play a role along with others, and together that creates a whole. Analogous to asking ourselves about feelings, purpose, and a pattern to our lives, in role we inquire about the organization.

- *How do people talk with each other? For example, do they tend to be open, combative, curious, or polite?*

- *How does leadership identify the organizational challenges that people face? Examples: becoming more aggressive in the face of competition, dedicating itself to service.*

- *What do people at middle and lower levels identify as the organizational challenges? Examples: reducing ambiguity, showing more respect for people.*

- *How do the organization's structure and history shape its identity? For example, is it a family-owned business struggling to compete, a start-up on the cutting edge of technology, a public agency dedicated to underserved populations, or a series of mergers that diffuses focus?*

- *What is the organization's general outlook on the future? For example, is there excitement in the face of changing markets? pessimism about the future quality of work life?*

- *What are the urgent business needs? Examples: regaining market share, efficient transfer to a new service delivery system, cost reductions.*

- *What fears seem to predominate? Examples: that people are not "on board," that leadership is not tuned in, that the new technology will undermine service.*

- *How are these fears expressed in the way people interact? Examples: people are more guarded or distracted, people are trying to work together better, constant reference to crisis undermines morale.*

- *How do different parts of the organization express different concerns? For example, what are the concerns of marketing versus research and development, or middle managers versus line staff?*

   This extension of our inquiry invites us to think of the organization as an organism of its own, with many different parts, and then to consider what it means to be a part of that system.

What is the situation like in your own work environment, with regard to your role? How is your role an expression of who you are? Of the needs of the organization?

Stepping into Role

The most daunting occasion for attending to role, perhaps, is when we are moving into a new one. Many things require our attention, there are hidden barriers, and we know that others are watching our every move—at a time when we are usually least informed about the system we have just joined. We cannot do everything at once, of course, but where do we start? How do we proceed? And how can we make sure we don't lose ourselves along the way?

Cary has had twenty years of experience managing obstetrics units in hospital settings in different parts of the country. She has recently taken a position as director of a particularly troubled unit in a small rural hospital. Less than a month into her new job, she describes her patience as razor thin. In the last week, the human resources director insinuated that he had to do her job for her, and the finance officer demeaned one of her nurses over pay sheets. Her own staff have been resistant to her every move, and one nurse made an offhand remark that they've seen directors come and go, implying that the staff knew what was best. Cary has been told by the person she reports to that she needs to clean up the mess left by the last director. She wants to get started, but all she has done is react to problems. "It seems that for every rock I kick over, five snakes come crawling out." Troubled but not beaten, Cary begins to make her initial assessment of what truly matters in her role. She decides she will focus on developing the clinical competence of her nurses and changing the tone of communication to one of support and mutual advantage. She knows she is in for a rough ride and she knows from experience that she will have to take it one day at a time.

Cary's story is a reminder that we don't start in a new role with a blank sheet of paper. In the following pages, we'll explore ways of stepping into a new role, and in the next chapter, we'll examine some ongoing practices for being effective in role.

AUTHORS' NOTE ON ROLE AND NONTRADITIONAL EMPLOYMENT

We recognize that in the many forms of employment today, there is a continuum of involvement in organizational life. How we think about role does not depend upon a traditional job structure, however. The contract programmer showing up at her per-diem client site must still consider how she wants to bring herself to the position for which she is contracted. The single-practitioner psychotherapist must still consider how he might best take up his role with his patients, the interns he is supervising, and the colleagues that form his professional network. As authors, our assumption is that you will reflect on the relevance of this material for your own situation and apply it accordingly.

What Are Our Intentions?

When stepping into a new role, it's crucial to ask yourself about the desired outcomes of your efforts. Though the question may seem simple and straightforward, it holds the link between the person—everything about who we are—and the needs of the organization. And our response becomes an expression of our *intentions*—how we intend to be and what we intend to do in our role.

Intention requires us to wrestle from the very beginning with the person-position duality. The inquiry into our intentions requires an almost back-and-forth motion of related questions that sift through the first layer of our understanding: *What are my needs? What are the organization's needs? What are my strengths and weaknesses? What are the organization's strengths and weaknesses?*

What are my reasons for moving into this role? What are the organization's reasons for wanting me in this role?

An outcome of wrestling with these questions is greater clarity about how we might make a meaningful contribution. We end up in roles for a variety of reasons—we're chosen because of prior experience, or we're following someone who's been promoted, or it's the next logical step in our development. At another level, it may be that we ended up in a particular role to avoid something else, or because others either overestimate or underestimate our talents. And though these reasons may explain how we got into a role, intention requires a deeper level of understanding. In that sense, intention is related to purpose: What will be the overarching purpose that guides how I make decisions in this role?

In taking up a new role we dream and fear the extremes of what might be possible. Sonja, for example, has just been promoted to an area supervisor position in a school district known for poor morale and ineffectiveness. She is acutely aware that reformers view the *old guard* as overly bureaucratic, with a status quo mindset. And given her seniority in the system, she too could be suspect. Rather than feeling defensive, her understanding of intention allows her to see the new position as an opportunity to demonstrate visible leadership. The very first images of herself in the new role, therefore, include spending more time at school sites than in her office, actively promoting a new attitude among administrators and teachers.

Intention is also related to integrity, in the sense of its cohesiveness. We don't always get to do what we want in an organizational role. Our intentions are complicated by the real politics of our organizations. We may want to develop the potential in every person, but some people may simply not work out. The integrity is about whether we can return to our intentions: When we cannot fulfill our intentions in a given situation, can we know them well enough and be grounded in them enough to figure out how to return to them? In that way, intention is expressed not so much in any single action as in how the actions add up. Furthermore, intention is not just a mental strategy or an abstract purpose; rather, it is embodied, reflected in the tone of voice and physical presence. People are reading you, not just your words.

Alan's Story

I REMEMBER READING in the paper about a meeting between Oakland Mayor Jerry Brown and a group of African American ministers over a contentious staff issue early in his administration. One of the ministers reported that the group had been very blunt with the mayor, and that the mayor had been flustered and at times inarticulate responding to their concerns. Yet the minister also said that there was a "fire" in Brown, which convinced the minister and his colleagues that, in spite of the differences, he was someone they could work with—someone they believed would truly listen to them and whose actions would somehow reflect their concerns, even if they didn't get exactly what they wanted. For me, the minister's comment suggested that Brown embodied a solidity and clarity that transcended their differences as well as Brown's visible discomfort. Intention, in this case, meant neither acquiescence nor rigidity, but instead a steadfastness in how he would approach various issues as mayor. ❧

Whatever we want to call it, whether clarity of purpose, fire in the belly, or integrity, intention is about focus and energy and steadfastness—a presence that is sensed by others.

Reflection
PERCEIVING INTENTION

In your current role, a new role, or one you are assuming as part of your current responsibilities, reflect on the following.

- WHAT ARE your needs? What are the organization's needs?
- WHAT ARE your strengths? What are the organization's strengths?

- WHAT ARE your weaknesses? What are the organization's weaknesses?

- WHAT ARE your reasons for moving into this role? What are the organization's reasons for wanting you in this role?

Given your responses, take a step back and reflect for a moment on the implications for your intentions. Whatever clarity you may already have, try to open to any new insights. When you are ready, continue.

- WHAT INSIGHTS do you have about the outcomes you desire for your role?

- WHAT STANCE or actions will you take to move toward these outcomes?

HONING OUR INTENTIONS

Intention is something waiting to be revealed, in layers. Our intentions are a mix of light and dark. By opening ourselves to the question of intention, we bring up from the bottom some of the darker elements that we need to understand as part of the mix: We may start with our best intentions, such as service to others—then we get in touch with the more self-serving motivations or our need to dominate or be right. Honing our intentions, therefore, is an ongoing practice that goes deeper over time and in concert with our openness.

When we step into a new role, there are more questions than ready solutions; but we can't wait for all the answers. We recognize that we're at the bottom of the learning curve and that we are reacting to our understanding of others' expectations. Yet to avoid becoming captive to others' expectations, we need to begin translating our intentions into actions. We are creating our own roadmap—one that we construct for ourselves out of our understanding of the territory and how others respond to us.

First Actions

Inevitably when we act, what is noticed is not just our actions, but the process and tone and means we use to achieve our ends. Roger, for example, recently assumed the leadership of a research division for a food and beverage company. Uncertain about the specific contribution he might make, he found that he cared a great deal that the research group's contribution should be directly relevant to the company's strategic business needs. As part of understanding the group and how he might approach his role, he interviewed all the senior researchers. To his surprise, he found a vacuum of consensus about the reason for the group's existence and its relation to the company's business. At the next research leadership meeting, Roger raised the issue several times, until the others agreed that they should meet again to discuss their vision. When they met again, Roger opened discussions by introducing a few key philosophical questions about the group's relation to the company, after which he turned the meeting over to others to take the lead in more specific discussion areas and next steps.

By conducting interviews and discussing what he found, Roger declared his intention to others in the research group—that he cared about the group's connection to the company's strategic business needs and that he valued others' perspectives. By teeing up the vision meeting and then turning it over to others, he demonstrated his intention as a leader—that he would lead strategically, with questions, versus controlling the entire meeting, and that he would allow others to grapple with the questions, deepen their own understanding of the issues, and take responsibility for actions going forward.

To put a twist on the story, let's imagine that Roger is hired as one of the senior researchers. How might the story play out differently, in terms of translating his intentions into first actions? If we focus on the other researchers as his group of peers, we might imagine Roger working in collaboration with his boss on the question of the group's strategic relation to the company. Assuming that his boss does not feel threatened and agrees to Roger's interviewing his peers, he might even allow Roger to set up a separate meeting to discuss the issue—or not. And the peers may be excited about the subject—or they may resent Roger. There are many different scenarios for how Roger's passion for connecting research to company strategy might play itself out. He may find that others are open toward him and his focus on strategy, or he may find that he is allowed to express that intention only within his specific area of research.

The complexity of how others might receive our actions highlights role as an expression of ourselves *in relation*. When stepping into role, we must be aware of the extent to which we are *authorized* to act by others, including not only our supervisor but also others in the system. To some extent, we must authorize ourselves as we step into role; doing so allows us to be creative in our approach to role and perhaps to accomplish what has not been possible before. Yet, authorization and self-authorization are always mediated by the fact of our actions being in relation to others. The idea of conscious communication implies a realization that every action sends some kind of message to others.

ON AUTHORIZATION, SELF-AUTHORIZATION, AND CONSCIOUS COMMUNICATION

AUTHORIZATION: *Positions are linked with* authorization—*the "commission" given to us by the organization and backed with the support of various resources. Over time, we become aware of how we're authorized by the system. Usually some aspects of our authorization are straightforward—what we're told is the way it is—and other aspects are not. The mystery of organizations is finding the boundaries of our authorization before venturing out too far and tripping over a land mine: Do we have the authority to call a meeting of peers, for example? Can we order supplies without going through channels? Can we initiate a new project idea? Can we challenge a superior's assumptions, or even his or her style of interaction? In an environment of teams, task forces, and more loosely knit organization structures, the question of where our authorization begins and ends is ever more ambiguous and requires more testing out. In taking first actions, therefore, be aware that there will be reactions suggesting where other people think your authorization lies. Be prepared to negotiate, knowing that how you communicate is how others will start to understand you in role.*

SELF-AUTHORIZATION: *You may invent new ways to act in role based on how you authorize yourself. There's a creative tension between position authorization and self-authorization: You may be able to do things in a role that others have never done before, and you wouldn't know that unless you test it out.*

CONSCIOUS COMMUNICATION: *When stepping into a new role, conscious communication takes into account who we are, what messages we want to convey, and how we communicate the message. How should you present yourself at the staff meeting, for example? Even when you are in a new role with the same group of people, they will hear you and see you differently than when you were in your previous role. Being new to a role also makes us highly vulnerable to stereotypical assessments: A male supervisor in a health department was perceived as being blunt in his interactions; the mostly female staff nicknamed him "Adolf." And we can also be careless about something as basic as our tone of voice, paying little attention to how we come across. Be mindful, therefore, about what impression you'd like to convey and how best to deliver it: Being silent may be seen as disagreement or disinterest; being assertive, however, might be viewed as taking the issue away from those who are working with it. Consider asking some questions of yourself as preparation for conscious communication:* Do I want to convey caring? Do I have knowledge of the pressures people are facing? Do I want to speak outright about what I intend to bring to the role?

As with intentions, there is a layering of understanding about authorization and communication that takes time to untangle. We begin immediately, with a kind of chronicling of our experience in the first weeks and months. As we gather data about the system, we begin to develop a larger view of it, and we pay close attention to any *patterns:* How do people interact with one another? Are they indirect or overly obedient? Do they say the "right" things but everyone knows they think something else? Or do they chew things to death? The patterns inform us about how best to take up role, because we do it in relation to other people and their roles.

Application
Data for the Road Map

Once we've had some initial experience in a role, we can begin to draw on that experience to answer questions we couldn't answer earlier. We may no longer be groping in the dark, yet there is still much that is new, much that needs to be understood. In this still-early phase of stepping into a role, we have enough information to begin to construct a map for ouselves. The questions in the next application are intended to be less an inventory and more an opportunity for allowing major concerns and insights to emerge, in terms of both our person and the position. It helps to revisit these questions periodically, since they can't always be answered immediately, and to allow our responses to deepen and continue to inform us as we go along.

Questions We Need to Ask Ourselves

Interviewing Ourselves	*Examples from People in New Roles*
How best do you learn? Reflect on how you might dive into a first assignment.	I learn by getting a hold on tangible things. If I can get something in my hands to read, that helps me know if I'm covering the bases. I also learn from experience. I'm not good with abstractions.

Interviewing Ourselves	*Examples from People in New Roles*
What do you think are the reasons you were chosen for this? Think about your strengths, but go beyond. Why else might you be seen as the one for this role?	I'm not sure. I think the person who hired me trusts me. I think that's because I do what I say I'll get done, and she knows I value client service. It's still somewhat of a mystery to me, though.
What do you fear, or what do you have problems with? Think about what aspects of this role evoke insecurity or what situations feel most uncomfortable.	I have trouble thinking on my feet. I'm not comfortable with ambiguity, and I don't know the specifics of people's jobs, such as the controller's, or the one scheduling. The technology is foreign to me. Also, I don't have the organizational knowledge—how large groups make decisions or how to boost morale and also get the work done.
What were you told would be your areas of engagement? Think about the specific assignments or areas of responsibility that have been identified for you. Consider how these areas seem connected to or fragmented from each other.	Five areas, including liaison with a reengineering program for one of the departments, monitoring the costs of outside resources, and orientation of new employees. With the exception of employee orientation, none of the initial areas are very hands-on, and that makes me uncomfortable.
What do you most care about? This gets at values, including what kinds of values embody your approach to work efficiency, competitive edge, inclusiveness, intelligence, service, and so on.	Really good teamwork is important, and that the organization is financially viable, and of course, how our customers get treated—caring, along with technical help.
What stories, direct or indirect, typify your experience of the organization? Think about what the story might mean regarding relationships and different roles. What further questions arise?	When I first started teaching in an urban middle school, I witnessed an argument between a teacher and the janitor over keeping toilet paper in the girl's bathroom. Afterward, the other teachers all congratulated her (the teacher) for sticking to her guns. I thought, "What kind of power do the janitors have here? And what about the teachers?"

Interviewing Ourselves	Examples from People in New Roles
Looking back on this three years from now, what do you think will allow you to be successful? Take a step back from the everyday issues, to think long-term.	I think it might have to do with not responding to everything as if it's a crisis, and explaining the reasons for decisions. And remaining visible.

Understanding Patterns in Organizations

Examining how people think and behave helps us to continue to fill in the map we're creating of the organization. We began looking at these issues with basic questions about the organization, and we gathered more clues from the chronicling of our early experiences. Focusing on patterns, connections, and tendencies reveals the next layer of understanding we need in order to make sense of the organization and how we might construct our role.

PERCEIVING SOCIAL PATTERNS

To recognize patterns, it helps to be aware of the full range of our experience and the data that we've gathered, but then to step back for a softer, more curious, less direct view. The following are examples of the kinds of questions that can quicken our insights about an organization's patterns.

- *What is the emotional life of the organization? Examples: fragmented, warm, demanding.*

- *How are people appreciated? Examples: through gatherings with food, acknowledgment of group achievements, praise in one-to-one meetings.*

- *What's the real attitude toward the customer? Examples: the customer is central or a distraction, worthy of advocacy or too demanding.*

- *What's the nature of competition and collaboration? For example, is sharing information viewed as extra work or central to being effective? Is the tone of interaction about showing your competence or seeking help and support when appropriate?*

- *Within the system, are there distinct cultures, competencies, tasks, or challenges that distinguish groups from each other? Examples: the back office versus front office, leadership groups versus line people.*

- *Are there secrets or stereotypes that go unaddressed? Examples: sexual liaisons, abusive behavior, discriminatory practices.*

It is not so much any one specific question in this lineup that is so crucial as it is the depth of thought that it takes to move through them as a totality. By reaching for these clues, we approach a comprehension of the obvious and not-so-obvious elements of the system we've joined. From that point of understanding, perhaps we can determine how best to enter into it.

What insights do you have about the patterns in your organization? What new patterns are trying to emerge?

Eventually we learn that a role is something we continually create for ourselves. While some aspects of the role are handed to us, others may be withheld until we negotiate them, hidden from us until our understanding deepens, or nonexistent until we create them. We are continually learning about the organization and its needs, as well as our authorization and what's possible. There is not just the opportunity for self-authorization, but the necessity of it. Without some degree of *imprinting* ourselves into the role, the role will never truly be ours but will remain a mere position. Chapter 9 continues our discussion of role, focusing on specific disciplines we need for being effective in role on an ongoing basis.

9

Practices for Being Effective in Role

A MOTHER GOES IN to wake up her son. "Johnny, get up, it's time to go to school." Johnny moans, "But I don't want to go to school. The kids hate me, I don't get along with the teachers, and the food is bad. Give me one good reason why I should go to school." Johnny's mother says, "I'll give you two. First, you're forty years old. Second, you're the principal."

The humor of the punch line points to how difficult role can be. While stepping into role is a challenge in its own right, being effective in role on an ongoing basis presents a different set of issues. *Showing up* with our full range of selves, for instance, is a practice that takes discipline. We chuckle at Johnny's wanting to hide under the sheets, because we recognize that longing, to just be "free of all these responsibilities."

Other practices essential for being effective in role, the focus of this chapter, include retrieving the pieces of ourselves that get lost along the way, resisting the forces that would pull us away from our role, learning to work with ambiguity, and stepping back to discern what's going on.

In contrast to specific skills that we may draw upon for certain tasks, each of these practices functions as a discipline to be applied to our unique situation. As our appreciation for each practice deepens, we develop a diffuse kind of awareness that carries over into each particular situation. We may not consciously concentrate on staying in role, but we notice immediately when we are being pulled away from it; we may not enjoy an ambiguous or conflicted situation, but we can learn to appreciate the opportunity for sharpening our understanding.

There is no magic formula for developing these practices. Our hope is that you will filter the material through the lens of your own experience and apply it as appropriate to your situation.

Showing Up

Sitting in a breakout session as part of a conference on facilities planning, Meg found herself only half-listening to the conversation. Although this early part of the session was supposed to be about introducing yourself, two men had already started discussing the subject matter. Meg was feeling overwhelmed and distracted. When someone finally noted she had not yet checked in, she paused and into the ensuing quiet said, "Well, I think that's because I've checked out." She explained that she was feeling worried about some conflicts at her office and that the early conversation in the room had felt distancing and abstract. Yet, she said she really wanted to be at the session and thanked the group for listening to her. The effect of her words was sobering. Others began to observe and speak of their own genuine feelings and to engage more personally in the subject they had come to discuss.

What Meg did so skillfully was bridge her own interior world with the work of the session. To show up, we must first be honest with ourselves about what parts of us are present and what parts absent, what we honestly look forward to and what we resist or fear. Paradoxically, when we can acknowledge what is difficult, we can better attend to our responsibilities, with greater resolve to be real. And in doing so, we have a remarkable effect on others to do the same.

To *show up* means to bring ourselves fully to a role. In Linda's story about producing a movie, in chapter 7, she recognized that her dream was achievable but that she would have to go face-to-face with her fears and learn to move through them. By including her fears consciously, she kept them from sabotaging her. A large part of overcoming obstacles, for Linda, had to do with the relational aspect of role—that if she were to be a producer, she would need an experienced mentor, a production crew, a cast, and financial supporters. She overcame her distaste for networking by seeing it as part of the dream. "Holding the goal sacred" became Linda's mantra for showing up every day.

It's important to pay attention to how we show up with others: Do we tend to roll forward like a bulldozer, or are we alert to how others receive us? Are we receptive to what others have to offer? When others sense that we are fully present for them, they tend to reciprocate, showing up more themselves and hiding less.

How do you show up in your role? What aspects are you reluctant to bring with you? What impact do you have on how others show up in their roles?

Recovering What Gets Lost

The good news of stepping into role successfully and learning to show up is that we are in a better position to bring more of our selves to bear on the role. The bad news is that, in doing so, we face risks. *What if I'm wrong? What if my efforts aren't appreciated? What if others are critical?* Inevitably when we are in role, we suffer some degree of loss or wounding, because bringing ourselves forward, we learn that others do not always appreciate all of what we bring.

The losses most often are so subtle that we don't notice them happening. Perhaps it's an inclination to hold back that begins when our sense of humor drops away. In situations where senior people dictate, we may lose confidence in our own decision-making ability or capacity to analyze. Perhaps we feel inclined to stifle all of our feelings about sexuality—including the desire to be noticed or to be playful. In a setting where there is little regard for intuition, we may lose regard for our own. Maybe others don't seem to care about justice as much as we do. We begin to participate less energetically in meetings, our passion for a change effort drops away—or, to the contrary, we get carried away with our opinions to the point that we become impatient with others and stop listening. And at some point, we realize we have gotten lost.

The reality of being in role means risk—that in the confinement of a particular role, pieces of ourselves may get left behind. The problem is not so much that we lose pieces of ourselves, for that's to be expected. Rather, the problem lies in our ability to call the pieces back. How do we *re-collect* our sense of humor? our ability to make decisions? our playfulness?

Sometimes the loss stems from an insult. Brian is an executive coach to Gordon, a young, bright, and energetic CEO of a start-up software company. At times, Gordon is calm and sensible, and at other times he seems caught up in an impossible whirlwind of chaos. In one of their coaching sessions, Brian felt himself being pulled into the chaos and struggled with how best to respond to a question by Gordon. He began his answer with the words, "Thinking out loud about this . . . ," when Gordon cut him off. "Don't do that," Gordon told him. "You don't do it well." Brian resisted being defensive and instead asked Gordon for his thoughts. He knew intellectually that Gordon's cutting him off was "data" about Gordon and his need for coaching. Emotionally, however, he felt dazed; the comment stung, and he felt like getting revenge. He felt so dazed, in fact, that he lost any sense of being able to coach Gordon. How could he think about coaching, when all he wanted to do was strike back?

Brian took some time to reflect on the situation. If there was one thing he could feel secure about, he told himself, it was his ability to think silently or out loud. There's no need to take it personally, he tried to reassure himself. The insult pointed to Gordon's leadership style and the impact he had on others around him. Yet it was personal, and it hurt. There was a wounding— not just from the insult itself, but in the way he lost his ability to be effective in his role as coach. In anger, Brian imagined informing Gordon that he refused to work with someone so carelessly and inappropriately insulting.

As his reflection deepened and the recovery process continued, Brian began to have more compassion for the chaos in which Gordon admittedly felt trapped. Brian concluded that he needed to address the insult but didn't want to make it a personal issue isolated from their work relationship. Instead, Brian saw it as a useful example for illustrating to Gordon how he might have inadvertently insulted others and made himself subject to subtle forms of revenge or retaliation.

In their next session, Gordon talked about difficulties with his management team, and Brian told him about his experience in the previous session. This proved very helpful to Gordon, who was struggling with what seemed, until that moment, veiled forms of animosity and resistance from his management team. The impact of the insight was sobering, and Gordon could now see how his behavior undermined his position with the team. Without making it personal or getting caught in debate, Brian used the experience of being insulted to coach his client.

Alan's Story

SOMETIMES THE loss stems from idealizing the competence of others. Andrea, a client of mine in a senior but ambiguous role within her organization, continually described her discomfort with her focus and contribution. Our conversations seemed to aid her, but I was left feeling that something very basic was still unresolved.

One day she came to our session with a fresh perspective on her role. She told me she had listened to historian Doris Goodwin's description of FDR—of how he believed he could live with his decisions if he felt that nine or ten reasonably intelligent people, given the same information he had available, would have agreed with him. I asked her what was significant about this. "Well," she answered, "he wasn't comparing his decision making to Caesar or Alexander the Great—just reasonably intelligent people." And how did seeing this affect you, I asked her. "Well, I've been uncomfortable in this role because I keep thinking of people I respect, maybe even have on a pedestal, and think they would know much better than I what was really important. And now I think, 'Well, if I'm doing what a majority of reasonably intelligent people would do, I'm doing okay.' And that takes a big burden off my mind." ❧

The sting of insult Brian suffered is an experience we all recognize. And while we may not idealize others' competence in the same way as Andrea, we know about her fear—that there is someone else with the right answer, someone else who can do it better. It's a "dirty little secret," this tyranny that we all live with while trying to appear confident.

Perhaps you have already begun to reflect on how parts of your self in role have become diminished. Maybe you have recently lost a political battle or felt discounted or dismissed. In such moments, wounding and loss go hand in hand. In the practice of recovery, we attend to our feelings that something within has suffered or gone awry; then, with compassion for ourselves and others, we acknowledge the loss and appreciate what that piece brought to our lives.

Reflection
FINDING AND RETRIEVING THE LOST PIECES

- As YOU reflect on the difficulties you experience in your work role, are you aware of any pieces of yourself that feel diminished or lost?

- WHAT PIECE is missing, and what value did that piece bring to who you are?

- WHAT CAUSED you to forfeit that aspect of who you are?

- SIMPLY REMEMBERING these pieces that have been lost is an important part of bringing them back. Are you aware of any other ways that you can bring these lost pieces to bear on your effectiveness at work?

While some degree of loss and retrieval is ongoing, we can also learn to suspend parts of ourselves in the service of what we're trying to accomplish. It is not necessarily appropriate to reveal all aspects of ourselves all the time. Rather, we practice awareness and appreciation of our multiple selves within to the greatest extent possible, then consciously select from among them. *What's the need in this situation—the wise and knowing part of myself, my analytic side, or my gentle side?* It may seem overly idealistic to think we can manage this process, yet awareness of choice can significantly aid us in doing so. In this way, we find that we can bring ourselves fully *and* willingly suspend parts of ourselves.

One of the most dramatic examples of this was articulated by Desmond Tutu, reflecting on his experience chairing the Truth and Reconciliation Commission in South Africa. The commission's mandate was to document the horrors of apartheid and sow the seeds of reconciliation between blacks and whites. On the very first day, listening to the testimonies, Tutu was filmed crying. He realized afterward that his reactions would become the media's focus and determined not to allow himself to cry again at the hearings.

"I cry easily," Tutu later explained. But he believed that the rightful subjects of attention should be the victims of the horror, not his reactions. And by suspending his show of visible feelings, he redirected attention to where he believed the healing process was best served. When asked about his own grieving and healing, Tutu responded by saying that when he needed to, he cried at home or in church, and that he believed his capacity to cry was a gift—a sign of vulnerability and weakness that was part of a greater knowing, that one does not have all the resources within oneself. One is thrown back on God and the goodness of others that coexists with the horrors.

Tutu's story is a vivid example of being fully present yet making choices about what feelings are appropriate for a given situation. In suspending his show of feelings, he did not annihilate them, but cherished them and allowed their expression in the settings of his choice. We are unlikely to face such dramatic circumstances, but in small ways each day, we are faced with making choices about how to express ourselves without disowning the vulnerability and weakness within. To show up means to be truly present with others, respectful of both our inner world and the task we are engaged in.

> *There is a dual paradox of how we bring ourselves in role: The first is that we bring ourselves fully, aware that some loss is inevitable, but faithful to ourselves in the sense of returning to look for the missing pieces. The parallel paradox is that we suspend parts of our selves in order to be fully present to the task at hand.*

Staying in Role

Staying in role may sound straightforward, yet it's one of work's greatest challenges. The telephone rings, and once more we set aside our forecasting to listen to a friend's latest crisis, or we go into a meeting so upset about an e-mail that we sit silently, stewing. Whatever intention we may have held toward our role, it is quickly forgotten. As with the inevitability of losing pieces of ourselves occasionally, we can no less avoid being pulled out of role. Over time, however, we can learn to recognize more quickly when we've been pulled away and even to anticipate the pull. The following table summarizes a few examples of how this happens and what we might do about it.

Attending to What Pulls Us Out of Role

What pulls us out of role?	*How can we step back in again?*
CRITICISM Though there is nothing like criticism from others to take the wind out of our sails, more often the greatest distraction is from our very own internal critic. Criticism feeds into fear. . . .	BE COMPASSIONATE With *com-passion* (meaning "suffering with"), we "suffer with" what's pulling us out of role, acknowledging and working with our internal critic so that it is less destructive (see chapter 3 for ways to work with our Critic). It also helps to be compassionate toward any external critics, recognizing that others are sometimes caught in their own web of issues. The more we can attend to the *content* of the criticism and to how it hurts us, the easier it will be to reach some kind of resolve within and refocus our intention.
FEAR Whether we fear that we won't get *X* done in time, that things are slipping through the cracks, that we're not competent enough, or that others will be let down, many fears can be traced to the fear of rejection and feelings of shame.	STEP BACK INTO ACTION AGAIN We need to address the fear and understand its basis, *discerning* what needs to be done and, if appropriate, plan to do it. If it's about competence, for instance, it helps to know whether it stems from the "tyranny of knowing someone else can do it better," or whether we really do need to learn something—perhaps how to work better, either technically or personally. If it's about disappointing others, discernment helps us to reestablish our priorities, stay balanced, and let go of what we can't control.
TRANSITIONS Every transition between activities brings the opportunity for distraction, whether phone calls and e-mail between appointments or conversations on the way back from meetings.	MINIMIZE TRANSITIONS Transitions are difficult to avoid, of course, but our vulnerability to distraction can be mediated with awareness, discipline, and a more structured approach toward time management when necessary. Sometimes before regaining our sense of rhythm, we need to take some kind of action—perhaps connecting with our family, carving out time to return phone calls, or getting a good night's sleep.

What pulls us out of role?	*How can we step back in again?*
COMPETING ROLES The demands of another role, as well as competing demands within a role, may interfere with our focus. Our role as parent may at times interfere with work, or our role as a task force member may consume our interests and impose on our "real" job.	BE REALISTIC ABOUT OUR ROLES When we take on a role, we need to assess what it means in relation to other roles that we have in our lives. While all the categories in this table overlap to some extent, the point here is to be clear about what roles we can take on realistically. Overextending ourselves is an invitation for constant distractions and fears—especially of disappointing others. The best prevention is to assess our capacity, being careful to not overpromise and letting go where appropriate. Accepting our limitations, that we're not superhuman, we may need to back out of some commitments to allow more space for staying focused.
FATIGUE The physical demands of travel, as well as long and intense work hours, deplete our energy. When we feel a strong need to eat or sleep, it is difficult to concentrate on anything else.	RESPECT OUR PHYSICAL NEEDS With little encouragement coming from the workplace, it's up to us to look after our physical needs. In addition to maintaining our health and being aware of our physical limits, we might call it a day when we know that we are no longer productive or, alternatively, turn to less demanding tasks. Short periods of centering can help, whether a five-minute meditation or an easy walk outdoors. And we may occasionally need to change our circumstances, to lessen the demands on us physically.
LOSS OF PURPOSE Because purpose is not rigid but shifts naturally with the flow of time and circumstances, it is not something that we "find" once and for all. Often we are alerted to its absence by the drop in energy we feel toward work—especially toward our role.	NOURISH OURSELVES SPIRITUALLY We regain a sense of purpose by setting aside space in our lives to reconnect with our longings, our dreams, and our values—with what really matters to us. Consider taking a mini-sabbatical or a Sabbath—one or several days away in the country or in nature, preferably alone—specifically to allow time for reflection. Be mindful of "first principles"—the values that anchor you to what you care about in work and why you chose to take up your role. It may help to revisit the application at the end of chapter 7. Reexamine your intentions toward your role, and identify an action that expresses those intentions.

What tends to pull you out of role? What insights do you have about anticipating the pull, or stepping back in?

Working with Ambiguity

The idea of role often carries with it associations of decisiveness—the job description as the decisive word on what we will do, or the organization chart for clarifying who will make decisions for whom. In American culture, decisiveness tends to be especially idealized in leadership roles. In a classic scene from *Twelve O'clock High,* General Savage (Gregory Peck) has his driver stop the car just outside the demoralized air base he will command. Before meeting the men, he must decide what to do. The general lights a cigarette and stands looking onto the air base, thinking. After two short puffs, a determined look comes over his face. "All right, Sergeant," he announces to the driver, as he drops his cigarette to the ground. Then he stamps it out, turns around, and gets into the car. This image of taking charge says, cigarette out, decision made—obvious leader.

The idealization of decisiveness, however, stands in contrast to the reality of what it takes to be able to wrestle through complex issues. Role is different from a job description, in that it's dynamic, not static, involving more a mindset than a specific set of responsibilities. Though some aspects of role are clear-cut, many aspects require us to bring different and sometimes conflicting parts of ourselves to bear on complex situations.

Raymond, for example, is the founder and president of a company that markets software, data, and risk management research for the financial community. He started the company with the intention of avoiding the traditional hierarchy that he found such a hindrance at the company he left. He wanted to work with a group of employees who felt free to create new products and who felt a stake in the company's success. Consistent with his intentions, he met regularly with his initial twenty-five employees and eliminated all signs of hierarchy, such as elegant offices or dedicated parking spaces. Even his business card had only his own and his company's name, not his title of president.

But now, with the company less than a year in operation and already three times its original size, Raymond wonders if the hierarchy he feared is exactly what his company needs. Perhaps *he* is the obstacle to fast action and fluid coordination. Two of his largest investors have warned him that the company is vulnerable with just one senior executive, and the number of decisions that need to be made is overwhelming. Intellectually, he thinks it's time to hire a number-two executive, but emotionally he fears that adding another layer of management will create new problems. What would his role be, if he delegates the day-to-day management to someone else? And would that person care about the business as much as he does?

In the reality of today's work world, both management and operational responsibilities require us to consider multiple perspectives. Raymond is sorting out the future viability of his business, the efficiencies of a flat organization, and the business case for structure, as well as his own personal satisfaction with being in charge and the personal toll of such a load. His capacity to consider multiple options and the pros and cons of each require emotional and intellectual flexibility. Should he hire the number-two person from the outside or from within? How would staff relate to having a peer named as their boss, compared with an outside person whom they don't know? Or should he name a president and make himself the number-two person?

Raymond's willingness to question himself allows him to discern what matters most, even in the urgency of the situation. Meanwhile, Raymond begins to delegate more decisions to his staff and to invite them into the dialogue about future direction. Rather than forcing himself to appear decisive, he establishes the groundwork for making workable whatever decision is made. And in the process, he learns more from his staff about what is really needed. A consequence of moving beyond one-sidedness in our thinking is that we begin noticing the legitimacy of multiple perspectives and engaging others to do the same.

Ambiguous situations often evoke ambivalence—we feel damned if we do, damned if we don't. The challenge of ambivalence is to not be paralyzed by it, but to use it to look at a situation with new eyes. When the problems are uncertain, never mind the solution, our ambivalence tips us off that there's a complexity we need to pay attention to. If we can learn to value our feelings of ambivalence, we can draw energy from them for finding more creative solutions. If we can't deal with our feelings of ambivalence, we will have difficulty dealing with the ambiguity of complex situations. In this way, the linking of role with decisiveness presents a false image of role management—that we should always have things resolved ahead of time. Instead, if we recognize ambivalence as a source for creative energy, we find a new way of thinking about what it means to be effective in role.

Cheryl's Story

NANCY, VICE PRESIDENT of her sales group, arrived for her coaching session with me and announced, "I'm going to resign today." A bit stunned at her decisiveness but aware that something very painful must have occurred, I began to probe about what had happened. A disagreement with her boss had broken her image of him as the ideal, ever-supporting, protective mentor, and a decision he'd made left her feeling abandoned and embarrassed before her peers.

As we continued to explore the situation, Nancy confessed her ambivalence about resigning—that while it would certainly serve as a way to punish her boss, it would not necessarily serve her own best interests. At that point, we could use the ambivalence to examine alternative perspectives and actions. In discussing the different perspectives she could take, she also came to appreciate the dilemma her boss must have felt: "Well, I know he was between a rock and hard place," she admitted, softening in her stance. She also realized how her reliance on his support had evolved into an unhealthy dependence, hindering her from feeling that she could stand on her own merits and adding an unfair weight to his actions.

Finally, Nancy's appreciation for how ambiguous this situation was gave way to a series of ideas about handling it more creatively. She could ask her boss more about his perspective, for example, and explain why the impact on her was so difficult to accept. We worked at finding a couple of different solutions she could discuss with him that might represent a "win" for both of them. By the end of the session, she had identified a plan of action that included two or three possible scenarios and options, and by our next session they had made considerable progress together toward a mutually agreeable outcome. ❧

Sometimes we steam ahead, ignoring our own ambivalence and focusing on the wrong problem.

Alan's Story

RECALL A consultation with a client who presented to me a problem that he labeled *communication*—how best to communicate a new proposal on staffing to those on his unit who would be affected. As he recounted the situation, going back and forth between the merits and challenges of the different proposals he considered, I asked him to pause. I said I could see the communication problem and it had nothing to do with how to present it to his staff. He looked at me with skepticism and some interest. The problem, I said, was not yet with what to say but rather that he was still arguing with himself. There was a moment of silence, and then he burst out laughing. "Yes, that's right. How the hell should I know if this is going to work?" ❧

In each of us, quite often, conflicted feelings vie for the position of our "true" feelings or for the shape an idea will take. Sometimes we conceal these battles from ourselves by finding others we can disagree with; or we repetitively focus on obstacles outside ourselves that distract us and offer respite from our own conflicted feelings. It's a simple equation to say that we lose our confidence or humor or clarity as a consequence of organizational life; it's another thing to say that the loss is an outcome of being in conflict with ourselves. We are most vulnerable to sustained confusion when we deny one side of our ambivalence or ignore the tension between the two sides. Rather than avoiding the awareness of conflict, we can foster a creative response by working with ambiguity, both within ourselves and the larger organization in which we take up our role.

Are you faced with any situations that pull on you to be decisive, and yet you are aware of more that needs to be understood? What might your ambivalence be teaching you about the situation?

Discernment

Similar to the way we have learned to approach the soul indirectly, we need to take a view from a step back, on occasion, to stay effective in role. Perhaps we are clear about our role, or perhaps we have questions. As with our sense of purpose, the clarity is important; then letting go of the clarity is important. Discernment is about stepping away from what we know and understand, stepping back to gain a perspective that can include insights not visible at close range.

The need to let go applies not only to understanding our role as a whole, but each situation we encounter while we are *in* our role. Discernment teaches us that each situation is new. While experience is a great teacher, we need to release the lessons learned from their imposing themselves upon us. But why is this necessary, we might wonder, if a situation seems clear-cut? Why not draw on earlier solutions? Because it is in exactly such cases that we are most vulnerable to being misguided by assumptions and solutions that may have been entirely appropriate at an earlier time. We do not necessarily abandon previous learning; yet we open to other possibilities. Approaching each situation as its own mystery allows us to stay creative, sharpens our perceptions, and allows us to incorporate new insights as we develop in our role.

> *Discernment is about going into that level deeper in our understanding, going beyond what we consciously know and take for granted, and opening to any insights that may emerge from the shadows.*

Discernment is the softer, more insightful version of analysis. Whereas analysis is aided by direct light, discernment comes by way of a softer light—like candlelight, which illuminates both beauty and shadows not readily visible in daylight. Stepping back from the intensity of analysis, discernment is about the more subtle, diffuse patterns. An analysis of a contentious meeting, for example, might attribute it to poor communication and inadequate options. Discernment might say, "Not only did people in the meeting tend to chew the issue to death, but I notice that happening a lot. . . . It seems to go along with a reluctance to take a stand for action, maybe because when there is failure, someone gets blamed."

Application
THE PRACTICE OF DISCERNMENT

As you prepare to write in your journal, consider a situation in which a deeper understanding would be helpful. Perhaps your boss has made a decision that contradicts information you've given her, or perhaps you find yourself caught in perpetual conflict or unable to make a decision. Ready? Writing the first answer that comes to mind, move through the following questions as quickly as possible. For this application, it is important to record your responses, as we will be reviewing them later.

- DESCRIBE THE situation.

- WHAT ARE the obvious issues?

- WHERE HAVE you seen a similar situation before?

- IN WHAT ways might this situation be different?

- ASSUMING THAT there are other issues behind the obvious ones, what might they be? Try to capture as many as six or eight perspectives.

- CIRCLE THE perspective you like the most, and put a check by the perspective you like the least.

- FOR YOUR favorite perspective, what other issues might it obscure?

- FOR YOUR least-liked perspective, what merits might emerge from hiding?

- TRY TO let go of your attachments to liking or not liking any of the perspectives, as well as to any ideas or concerns that may dominate your thinking, and jot down any other thoughts that come to mind.

Take a step back now, pausing for a moment to clear your mind. Acknowledge any thoughts that come up, then let them go. When you feel ready, look over your responses to the preceding questions and continue.

- DO ANY patterns or tendencies stand out to you, or things that may seem particularly important in the situation?

- WHAT REMAINS a mystery, or what might be worthy of further consideration?

- PAUSING AGAIN to reflect, do any other insights come to mind?

Consider taking a break, perhaps with a cup of tea or a walk. Allow your insights to turn over in your mind and in your heart. When you are ready, record in your journal your deepened understanding of the situation.

Keep in mind that insights do not necessarily appear on demand. They tend to emerge, sometimes slowly. Over the next several days, be aware of your thoughts and try to stay alert to any new insights as they emerge.

In these last chapters, we have considered role as the coming together of the person and the position—an expression of ourselves in relation with others. Continuing to move outward in our journey, from the "base camp" that is our inner wilderness to being effective in organizational roles, in the next chapter we consider our relationships to groups. Thus we turn our attention toward another kind of mystery, one in which we find ourselves to be both whole as individuals and part of a larger whole, inevitably connected to the souls of others.

10

The Emotional Tapestry of Group Life

IN THE PAINTING *La Danse* by Henri Matisse, a circle of people with joined hands dance in a ring. We cannot see their faces, yet we do not need to. Something familiar in the image reaches into our core, reminding us of what it means to be part of a circle, to be joined with others—to belong. It is as if the painting expresses a fulfilled longing—to belong in such a way that leaves us free, happy, dancing. This may contradict reality, where "belonging" can come at a cost to our individuality that rarely makes us want to dance. In our lives, we often struggle with what it means to participate meaningfully in work groups, family, or social circles. In our hearts, however, we long to join freely with others, without constraint.

The longing to belong is part of our nature. As social creatures, we know who we are by our interactions with others—by how others see us, by how we are similar and different, and by how we influence and are influenced by others. Our experience in groups, beginning with our families and extending into each new group we encounter, shapes and textures who we are. Though soul is an idea often associated with our uniqueness, group life is the crucible in which our character gains uniqueness and depth. How we work with others—our ability to act in common cause, as well as our frustrations in doing so—tells us about this interactive aspect of our soul.

In this chapter, we extend the inquiry of soul into the circles of connection around us. How can we account for the creative and constructive aspects of group life, as well as the deadening and destructive elements? How can we reimagine groups as living entities that we help create? How do we learn to trust our own instincts? How can we learn to work with vulnerability? And how do we learn about soul through participating in groups?

The Power of Groups

The power of a group lies in its collective capacity to bring out the best in us, to accomplish what no one individual can do, and to connect us in the most personal way to meaning and purpose. When a group's task resonates with our highest values, it can bring the transcendent into our lives. Religious groups tend to be powerful experiences, connecting people through spiritual beliefs and social practices. Part of the allure of volunteer and nonprofit work is its appeal as a labor of love. Participation in any group that focuses on breakthrough discoveries or significant achievements has a similar appeal—that our efforts are noteworthy. As authors joined in writing this book, we often have the sense that the book itself transcends both of us—as if the book is a third entity, using us to write itself. A significant aspect of group life, therefore, is the way an idea or a project takes on an importance that transcends any one element, allowing us to experience the power of "being in service to. . . ."

Cheryl's Story

A FEW YEARS ago, I consulted to the redesign effort of a chemical corporation in which several design teams, made up of a cross section of employees, were commissioned to redesign their respective plant or corporate function. One of the plant teams had struggled along in the analytical process and was now up against a firm deadline, yet they wanted to present their best work to the steering committee. For the final four days of preparations, they decided to lock themselves in a room at a nearby hotel until they were finished. And that's what they did. Working until 1:00 or 2:00 in the morning, sometimes in shifts, and ordering a lot of pizzas, they kept going—not only through the four days scheduled, but through the weekend as well. I was not consulting with this particular team, but I heard that by the time they went home on Sunday afternoon, they were not only well prepared, but euphoric—to the point that their consultant feared utter disappointment if the steering committee had questions or doubts.

Just before the presentation, the team members agreed they needed to let go of decisions not theirs to make and to remain open in the face of questions or concerns. At the presentation, the steering committee did express some concerns and requested further inquiry on a couple of issues, yet they were very impressed, both in terms of the content and the sense of commitment behind it. A few weeks later, even with some potential complications, the steering committee agreed to implement the design team's recommendations. With their collective achievement transcending what anyone might have guessed, some design team members counted the experience as the highlight of their career. ❧

In your own work life, what represents your most powerful group experience? What was the feeling like, being in this group? What motivated the group to achieve its task?

The focus on the constructive aspect of group life is but one side of the coin. Just as we discussed the shadow aspects of the individual, we must also contend with the shadow of groups. The comedian George Carlin tells audiences he doesn't like to join groups. They start with party hats, he explains, then get arm bands, and before you know it, they make up lists of people and start rounding them up in the middle of the night. Carlin's dark humor evokes the fear we have of the destructive side of the collective—not just in group life, in this case, but even in society. The destructiveness is particularly alarming when we realize that a group can sway individuals toward destructive action, even turning neighbor against neighbor. Individuals indicted for war crimes say they were following orders or were under extreme pressure, so swept away by the dominant group that they renounce personal responsibility.

In organizational life, the destructive potential of groups manifests itself in such forms as "groupthink," scapegoating, and ethics violations. It's been well documented, for example, that management groups, in an effort to smooth earnings and boost stock value, sometimes pressure accountants to manipulate the figures. In one highly publicized case, a large pharmaceuticals company purchased a software supplier, after which the merged company announced a series of earnings adjustments. This was followed by the disclosure of falsified sales at the software company, a drop in stock value of $9 billion in one day, and the dismissal or resignation of seven executives.[1] In such situations, one can imagine the destructive potential of several groups playing a role—the sales group needing to meet goals, the finance group expected to show favorable numbers to the prospective acquirer, management groups eager for a match on both sides, and merger accountants moving quickly to close the deal. Even those of us who invest in stocks and eagerly watch their growth share a collective responsibility for the pressure on companies to increase shareholder value. Many investors seem to care little about the methods a company uses to drive up the stock—until those practices touch their own careers and work lives.

The experience of a group's destructive potential is all too familiar. We feel its pull on us when we are asked to go along with something we believe is compromising, when we are pressured to approve a project we believe is ill conceived, or even when we participate in bashing management or exploiting our corporate privileges because others are doing it. Even more personally, we feel the destructive potential of a group when it stings us—when we learn about criticism circulating behind our back, for instance, or when we find ourselves targeted as a scapegoat so others can avoid taking responsibility themselves.

We have reason to be suspect of groups and organizations, therefore. Just as they can be creative, so can they ignore their effect on individuals and the environment while they pursue their goals. It is not that groups are either creative or destructive, but that all groups operate somewhere along a continuum, with elements of both present at different points in time. The challenge is to resist the trappings of one-sidedness—seeing the group as all-positive or all-negative—and, instead, to be aware of its complexity and where along the continuum we might locate our own participation.

Alan's Story

RECENTLY, I was asked to brainstorm with a planning team for a daylong program for middle managers. The topic of the planning session was how best to introduce the subject of spirituality at the event. The organization had always prided itself on being value-driven, and many in this group thought spirituality to be a timely subject. The conversation touched on numerous themes, including the importance of recognition, the message that employees are valued, and the values orientation of the company itself. Yet no specific suggestions were offered, and something seemed missing from the conversation.

Finally, someone noted that a man sitting toward the far end of the room was the person who worked most closely with the middle management group. What did he think? Trying to be diplomatic but honest, he talked about how difficult a period this had been for the company and that many of the employees were feeling cynical. And then he said, "When you can't live your values, you become someone else." His fear was that people would spend the day listening to speeches that didn't fit with their own experience and, worse, feel pressured to participate in small groups, knowing full well that what they said had little connection with their daily work lives. "The whole thing could be a charade." Past experience had taught him that words rarely led to new actions.

His words had a powerful impact. Many in the group agreed that what he was saying had much truth to it. One manager said that he had "named the pain," and another asked, "Whose responsibility is it to fix it?" A third manager suggested that managers in the event might reflect on their ambivalent feelings about the organization and speak from their own reflections. "We apparently need to deal with our own feelings of ambivalence," she continued. "Part of the problem is that the ambivalence is coming out as resentment, blame, and beating up on others."

As the group weighed these words, a new creativity emerged in the room. There was agreement that typical breakout groups with flip charts and group summaries should be abandoned. Through presentations and reflective questions, managers would be encouraged to consider their own experience; then they would have the opportunity to share their reflections, without any pressure to come to agreement or even to speak if they did not wish to. And in this way, it seemed to me that the dual nature of the organization and people's own mix of experience would be honored. ❧

The dualities of group life present a paradox for us as participants—that group life highlights both our highest aspirations and our basest instincts. Where we join in as individuals has everything to do with soul.

Are you aware of dualities in your own work group? In what ways are you pulled? Are there ways your participation might better honor the complexity of your group?

The dualities of group life take on special relevance when we consider a group as a living entity, with a complexity that mirrors our own. Learning to work effectively in a group is in fact similar to how we have learned to work with our own inner complexity. Understanding the group as a whole, and ourselves as a part of that whole, is our next vantage point for viewing the soul.

The Group As an Organism

We often think of a group as just a collection of individuals, or as a team if the individuals work fluidly with one another. Another way to think about a group is that it has a life of its own, with its own particular rhythm, its own personality, its own ways of creating behavior, its own instinct for survival. The complexities within a group play out in much the same way as our own multiplicity of selves, with some elements more dominant than others, some more conscious than others. And appreciation of these diversities moves the group toward its task.

We might imagine a group as having some of the same characteristics as a living cell. Like a cell, a group has a boundary that marks what is in and what is not. At this boundary, information and resources come in, while products and services go out. Within the cell, its parts, such as the nucleus and mass, are differentiated from one another. In addition, it may divide itself and multiply.

A group might also be understood as having certain dispositions or certain characteristics that serve as markers of an essential mood—that some groups are characteristically productive, sullen, needy, playful, demanding, intolerant, or overly analytic (as certain kinds of cells are characteristically toxic or healing or stabilizing to the body). Finally, a group can be thought of as having its own history, its own presence or spark of life, and its own orientation toward life beyond its own boundaries.

Cheryl's Story

THE UNIQUENESS of each group as its own life force has never been so vivid to me as in starting up four teams at an oil processing plant in Germany. For four days, the four teams were in one room with me, each group working around its own table and analyzing its respective set of assigned problems. One of the smaller groups tended to work very quietly and steadily, accomplishing a great deal. Another group argued so much on the finer points of analysis that it could hardly move forward on anything. Another enjoyed the experience so much that it tended to continually expand its task beyond what was realistic. And another group was childish, playing and wasting time during much of the productivity training, then shifting into competitiveness to impress their superiors.

Still, even with the remarkable differences between the groups, at another level it was possible to draw the lines differently and see the four teams as a whole. There was a commonality in the excitement and challenge they felt about their tasks, in the frustration of having other jobs to attend to, in the learning of new methodology for analysis, and in their desire to do well. In fact, by the end of our work together, the four teams had spontaneously organized their own interteam network to share ideas and experiences with each other as they continued in their twelve-week assignments. ✺

When examining group-level behaviors, we consider all behaviors as if they are an expression of the group. That is not to deny responsibility at the individual level. Rather, we are drawing the lines differently. Behaviors expressed by an individual, from this vantage point, represent the group. This does not mean that others in the group necessarily agree; on the contrary, often a group will use an individual to express something that others prefer not to deal with.

Russ, for example, was incensed that, for the second time in six months, a new leader was coming in to take over the lab. He had just gotten used to the last one. After a brief period with no department head, Nancy had been approved. Now she was sitting before the team, and Russ was fuming. Russ was especially angry that no one else seemed to be bothered about the situation. As he looked around, the others seemed to smile and make eye contact with Nancy—trying to get on her good side, he was sure. To his surprise, Nancy turned to Russ at one point in the meeting and said, "You seem angry." Startled and not quite knowing how to respond, Russ fumbled with his words; but she apparently did not want to have a dialogue with him anyway. "I'll bet you're not the only one who's angry," she continued, while turning her gaze to others around the table. The others had their eyes glued on Russ, whom they were secretly hoping would continue with the dialogue. As Russ began an attempt at explaining his anger, Nancy asked if he would mind not explaining. "I'd actually like to hear from the others," she said. "I understand I'm the second new department leader you've had recently. Fun, huh?" And she waited in silence.

Slowly, the others around the table began to hem and haw about the frustration of adjusting to new expectations. At first polite about what they liked and didn't like about the last leader, the conversation finally exposed some deep resentment about his departure. "I feel like he just used us," one colleague confessed. "He was just playing hard ball with this other company, until they got serious about a better position for him, and he never intended to stay here." Another expressed anger at management for not making research more of a priority, and another said she felt truly sad that they had lost a leader with great skills and experience.

As the discussion settled and they began to talk of going forward, Russ said he felt hopeful about the future. As if surprised by his own words, he admitted that he didn't feel as angry as earlier. "I guess it feels more like the load is shared, and that we might even be a better team this time around."

The transition Russ experienced, from anger to renewed hope, shifted along with the transition in the group, from acting polite to identifying and articulating concerns. The emotional load was shared, allowing for new thoughts and feelings to emerge. Groups "recruit" people for these types of emotional loads, perhaps based on individual affinities for certain emotions. Some of us, therefore, are more likely to express the anger that is in the group, the sadness, the frustration, or the joy.

Sometimes it's possible to trace how a certain role is passed from one person to another.

Alan's Story

ONE WOMAN told me of not wanting to be the one in her distribution office to keep expressing concern about the lack of communication with manufacturing. "I'm always the one out there on a limb." So she determined to just keep quiet about it. Soon, another person began to express a lot of frustration, as if picking up right where she had left off.

In another situation, an attorney had come to the conclusion that the firm's senior partners were putting them all in jeopardy and began to call meetings and rally people around what was wrong. When he attacked the integrity of one of the more trusted partners, he was told by his colleagues that he'd gone too far, and soon afterward he left. Within six months, however, another attorney had begun culling rumors and started to rally people around the problems with leadership, to the point where it seemed that it was the same behavior happening all over again. ❧

Sometimes a group will recruit two people to express polar ends of a dilemma, allowing the majority of the group to avoid dealing with it.

Cheryl's Story

IN CONSULTING to a small but expanding architectural firm, I was told of the interpersonal problems between two partners. One of the older partners was passionate about traditional hand-drawn plans, while a younger partner insisted that CAD (computer-aided design) was the way of the future. The firm had prided itself on its unique designs but was now undergoing financial stress in the face of a more competitive market.

In the conflict that was felt personally and painfully between the two partners, the firm contained its anxiety about whether new technologies would strip the firm of its creative juice. "Assigning" the struggle to these two partners allowed the majority of architects to think that they could keep the issue at bay and focus on their own work. But in reality, the entire firm was hindered by the voyeuristic diversion of attention to the fighting partners.

Once the problem was pointed out as an issue belonging to the entire system, others began to discuss the merits and limitations of each method, and the two partners stopped fighting. It is not that the dilemma was resolved immediately, but that the group finally took back its responsibility for the question. ✤

It is common to feel caught in a role we wouldn't necessarily have chosen. Perhaps it is to express all the anger, like Russ, or to voice the concerns for the group, or to rally people against leadership. Maybe it is the role of the pessimist, the provocateur, or even the one who can't understand. Or maybe the pull is toward taking charge of the group or making sure everyone feels okay. These are all ways that individuals take up roles on behalf of the group.

Reflecting on your experience, what roles have you tended to fall into, in your work groups? What roles do you prefer (or recruit) others to take up?

Scapegoating

Another group-level behavior is scapegoating, a common expression of collective shadow, used to help the majority of the group feel that the group is intact. The word *scapegoat* is drawn from a ritual that can be traced in some form to most ancient societies. In the early Hebrew tradition, the priests would symbolically transfer all of the wrongdoings of the people into a goat, then drive it into the wilderness, away from the community. In this way, there was some release from the difficulty of living according to the law, a key factor in their identity. Sending their collective guilt away with the goat allowed the Hebrew people to remain unified.

In today's workplace, scapegoating can be found in obvious as well as subtle forms. When an organization or a department seems to be threatened from within, by a particular member or subgroup, scapegoating may be the way the group attempts to preserve unity—by sending away the offending party. Though each situation is complex, indicators of scapegoating include the following:

- The tendency of groups to blame one individual or one department as a way to absolve others from responsibility, as in "Heads are gonna roll"

- A steady turnover of leadership—natural targets of projection, envy, and blame (see the section "Stepping into Role" in chapter 8)

- The blaming or mistreatment of administrative staff—easy targets because of their lower standing in the organization

- The firing or alienation of whistleblowers—often experienced as a live grenade

- The denigration of a particular subgroup on the basis of a perceived threat to the survival, viability, or performance of the organization

- The denigration of people behind their backs, without attempt to resolve the issue directly

- The alienation of those seen as deviant, perhaps because they challenge the system in a way that makes others uncomfortable

If not forced to leave, the scapegoat may be ignored outright, not taken seriously, or openly ridiculed. By being alienated rather than excommunicated, the scapegoat is allowed to roam within the ranks. But everyone knows that the scapegoat is to be shunned and will perhaps leave of his or her own accord.

Are you aware of other evidences of scapegoating, where placing blame upon an individual or subgroup helps the group to feel unified?

During a time of slowing sales and poor earnings, the regional office of an international training firm turned inward and destructive. Anxiety about sales shifted to general insecurity, short tempers, and finger pointing. The first to go were administrative support staff—one for performance, another for insubordination, and a third for violating firm policies. Next came whispers about professional staff not being up to snuff, along with a general reluctance to ask for help or to show support. Newer professional staff were quicker to be terminated, and no one felt particularly secure. Each time, it seemed the targeted victim became the current cause for the problems in the office—that if so-and-so were more on the ball, our sales would be higher. And rather than acknowledging the fear and insecurity that came with lower revenues, the office damaged its performance further by terminating competent associates. The insidious aspect of scapegoating is the sense of fragmentation, denial, and ill will that seems associated with this dynamic.

Scapegoating at the group level is comparable with rejecting certain aspects of our selves at the individual level. What is uncomfortable or difficult cannot be tolerated and is rejected. The rejected aspect of a group then becomes an obstacle to the group's further development. How can we think of a group as being whole, when suffering or blame is assigned to one member or a subgroup?

Furthermore, how can we think of ourselves as whole, if we are participating in scapegoating or even tolerating it? It is not that any individual is fully responsible for the group, but that each individual plays a part and must take responsibility for his or her own piece of an issue. Any one member's experience in a group reflects some part of ourselves, foreign as it may sometimes seem.

That is what it means to be part of the whole. Scapegoating denies this link.

For individual group members, the seduction of scapegoating is in the sense of relief, of not being held accountable. At the group level, the seduction is that if all the problems can be loaded into one individual, the group can feel unified. It is not unified, of course, because the underlying dynamics remain in the group, unrecognized. Thus the group will eventually seek another scapegoat.

BREAKING THE PATTERN OF SCAPEGOATING IS A MATTER OF SOUL

The ability to participate in groups without participating in scapegoating is directly connected with our wholeness. Recognizing that we do not live in isolation but are inevitably connected with the souls of others, we see how soul is tied to our participation in groups. As we have learned to retrieve and value aspects of our selves cast into the "shadow bag," so must we learn to acknowledge and work with aspects of others that are foreign to us. Our wholeness as individuals, therefore, is inevitably connected with the wholeness of the groups in which we participate.

As a member of a group, what can we do when we see that scapegoating is going on? It can be dangerous to draw attention to the victimization of the scapegoat, because you may draw the group's fire and become its next target. On the other hand, to protest by withdrawing from involvement—to be silent or to walk away from the group entirely—is to take on the role of another kind of victim or outcast. At times, leaving may be a necessary course of action, for self-preservation or building inner strength. But leaving does not usually help a group move toward wholeness.

Scapegoating may be countered by addressing the group's need for a scapegoat—by drawing attention, that is, to the issue the group is trying to avoid. In *naming* the shunned issue, we bring it into the group's conscious awareness. Even so, there is risk that the group will not be prepared to deal consciously with the issue and, instead, might prefer another scapegoat.

In a high-tech company positioning itself for e-commerce, the intensity of competition for market share led to scapegoating behaviors. Just as companies in the industry were springing up and disappearing, two software development directors in this company had come and gone. Martin, the third director, was struggling to establish his credibility. But in wanting to come across as a strong leader, he had been careless in his interactions with others, and that made him a good choice as a scapegoat victim.

A consultant suggested the pattern of scapegoating to Marcia, vice president of operations, and worked with her to find ways of addressing the problem. Under pressure to terminate Martin, Marcia decided to bring the group together to discuss the situation openly. She acknowledged Martin's weaknesses, particularly in some of his recent interactions, and pointed to his strengths as well, noting that one of his strengths was his willingness to look at his own limitations and to seek to improve. She asked the group if they could move beyond their current criticisms and allow Martin an opportunity to grow as a leader. She also pointed out what difficult times these were, that often people did not agree with each other about direction, and that any leader's success depended partly on the willingness of the group to be supportive.

Although the group took up the question seriously, the consensus seemed to be that Martin had lost credibility among key constituents, to the extent that even those who liked him felt that it was not a good situation for him to be in. There was almost unanimous agreement that Martin should step down. Rather than making a decision in the moment, Marcia said that she wanted to first speak with everyone individually. She wanted to put space between the group dynamics and how people felt personally, but further, she wanted individuals to start taking responsibility for their actions and to consider how they might better support leadership, even if it was going to be a new person.

After these individual meetings, she concluded and stated in a memo that it seemed to be in the best interests of the department and of Martin that he step down. But she would not appoint another director, she stated, until there was further reflection about how the group would support leadership to be more successful. While searching for a new director, she assigned all operational decisions to a group of managers who had reported to Martin. During this interim period, the management team came to appreciate the complexity of decisions and realized that in the future, decisions should not be on the back of one person. The story is still in process, but it seems the software development group is making progress toward owning its share of responsibility for the effectiveness of its leader.

Are you aware of any current situations of scapegoating in your work groups? What are the issues that seem to result in scapegoating? What steps might be taken, to move the group toward reflecting on the situation and responding in new ways?

Being Co-creators in Group Life

How is it that such strong patterns emerge in group life? How is it that a group develops such a unique identity? How does a group's "reality" get formed? How is it influenced? The questions challenge us, as we struggle to understand the groups we are a part of and how we might participate meaningfully, soulfully. In chapter 8, we spoke of stepping into role as depending a great deal on how we view the system we are in. So it is with our participation in groups, where our actions take on meaning against the backdrop of a group's creative and destructive power. To participate meaningfully in group life, we need some knowledge of the *perceived reality* of the group, the willingness to work with our own vulnerability in the face of that dominant reality, and the ability to discern which actions might have relevance. These are the themes of the remainder of this chapter.

So how *does* a group's reality get formed? Consider the following: If I believe that any act of kindness will be perceived by others as weakness or that only when I am loud and threatening will I achieve respect, I will behave accordingly. And if the system I am in continually reinforces these assumptions, I will stop seeing it as my perception and instead view it simply as reality. And if most everyone else in the system has a similar experience, then no one who comes in from outside can easily change this collective perception. This is what can be called *consensual reality*—a reality understood without having to be spoken out loud. And the linked behaviors—kindness treated as weakness, threats treated with respect—can be understood as behaviors emerging from this consensual reality or dominant story, the unspoken rationale for why certain behaviors are tolerated.

There is no way to fully escape consensual reality or behaviors tolerated by an unspoken belief system. Even in a short period of time, people brought together to contend with tasks and each other begin to shape a dominant story. We do this first in subgroups, checking to see who has similar perceptions or values or goals. And over time, certain beliefs begin to set in—that we are fair and decent or angry and cantankerous. We may even explain why certain behaviors are inevitable—that any business with high stakes and strong egos will inevitably have people jockeying for position and that you have to be tough to survive.

An implication of a group being its own organism is that, as a *part* of that organism, we are *subject* to its force. Being subject to a group means that we are vulnerable to its consensual reality or dominant story, much like a strand of seaweed is carried by the shifting currents: We may be anchored by the roots of our own individuality, yet we cannot help but be swayed by the currents of the collective forces. When we consider our vulnerability in this respect, the choice to join a group takes on greater significance.

Yet that's not the full story. Just as we may not be able to escape consensual reality, neither are we entirely at its mercy. Just as we are subject to things preexisting in the group when we enter it, so too do we have some capacity to influence it. We are not merely subject to our groups, therefore, but *co-creators* of them as well.

When we find subtle and not so subtle ways to challenge consensual reality within ourselves and our groups, we introduce the potential for healing and growth. Sometimes a simple question at the right time can open a group to think differently or move in new directions. Often, the real growth in groups lies in the counterstory—the cracking open of the collective mindset with a new reality. At a societal level, visionary leaders like Mahatma Gandhi, Martin Luther King Jr., and Nelson Mandela invited others to join in a new narrative that recognized mutual suffering and the promise of mutual advantage—*I have a dream.* . . . In the business arena, some leaders have begun actively pursuing their countervision of their respective industries, so that they are environmentally responsible as well as profitable. In each case, a discerning individual has challenged consensual reality with a counterstory and, with others, begun to create something new.

What counterstory in your work setting inspires you? When have you felt yourself to be a co-creator of group life? How might you take on the role of co-creator in a situation in your work life?

Creating a counterstory requires courage. How far can we go before being stopped by the prevailing norms and attitudes of the majority? How much can we risk? Do we need to fear our vulnerability, or is there a way to draw upon it as an internal resource for discerning and navigating the path of our participation?

Working with Vulnerability

In chapter 9, we saw that working with ambiguity is a key skill for being effective in role. In ambiguous situations, we draw energy from our feelings of ambivalence and use it to generate more creative solutions. In a parallel way, we find that learning to work with vulnerability is a key skill for being effective in group life. Attending to our vulnerability and that of others brings attention to a range of emotions within a group that can enhance or thwart its effectiveness.

In the story of the research lab, everyone in that situation was vulnerable in some way. Nancy, the new leader, demonstrated that she could work with her own and others' vulnerability, in several ways that moved the group forward. Had she not been willing to be vulnerable herself, she probably would not have had the courage to draw attention to Russ's anger or to invite the others to speak of their frustrations. And without appreciating others' vulnerability, she may have become impatient with Russ or delivered her expectations without pausing to hear from the others. Instead, she was disarming in how she opened herself to the concerns of the group. Nancy used vulnerability to cut through to some of the deeper issues.

A FEW POINTS ON VULNERABILITY AND GROUP LIFE

- *Though we do not normally think of feelings of vulnerability and effectiveness in groups as being linked, they are. Rather than taking us away from the work, feelings, as well as thoughts, are important for understanding ourselves and others. To think of a group as being effective without attending to feelings, therefore, is like working with one hand tied behind your back.*

- *Groups are always balancing the extremes of too much emotion versus too little—either being preoccupied with feelings to the point of disregard for the work, or disregarding feelings to the point that the work is lifeless.*

- *Expressing our feelings is not always the same as being vulnerable. Expressing our anger in a difficult situation, for example, may carry risk and require great courage, and we are certainly vulnerable. Yet the expression of*

> *anger may also be used as a defensive reaction to mask deeper, more fundamental feelings of fear, shame, or hurt.*
>
> - *People often show themselves through aggressiveness, the counterpoint to vulnerability. The aggressive patterns of proving, debating, and arguing tend to be about power based solely on dominating. We tend to hide our true feelings behind our view, our positions, our arguments, our facts, and our numbers. We may show anger or be calm, but our posturing covers up what's really bothering us or what's at stake. The issues that really matter aren't getting addressed.*
>
> - *Attuning to what makes us vulnerable allows for the art of thinking together. We may be unclear about our thoughts, or we have questions for which we don't have immediate answers. Revealing this kind of vulnerability invites others to join the process, to wrestle together with the issues and ideas.*

Sometimes our vulnerability can be about real danger. In the movie comedy *Analyze This*, Billy Crystal stars as an analyst treating a Mafia family leader, played by Robert DeNiro. DeNiro is in personal crisis because of panic attacks. He fears being brought down by feelings he doesn't know how to live with, and he knows that emotional weakness can be a death warrant. Concerned with an upcoming meeting of the Mafia families, he says, "In my world, I deal with animals, Doctor. And make no mistake about it, Doctor. Animals are very cunning and they sense weakness. I got less than two weeks to get stronger if they don't eat me up in the meantime."

The humor of the plot underscores a serious point, that there are dangers in group life and that any wounded animal is vulnerable to becoming prey. In our civilized work groups, we know too well that others can smell a weakness. If we feel that we're in danger, of course we have reason to not want to be vulnerable. In those situations, we must use our own judgment. There is no magic formula. If we sense danger, we need to keep our eyes open, pay attention, and avoid action until we reach a better understanding—which is what DeNiro did. On the other hand, if "danger" is our recurring story, we need to recognize that as a pattern and choose again to be open, to bring ourselves fully and risk being vulnerable.

If we can acknowledge vulnerability as an inherent aspect of soulful participation, then we can open to what there is to learn from it and tune ourselves by it. Instead of withdrawing in fear, for example, we use it as a cue: Is there something we need to attend to, that is so important that it seems threatening? When we can discern what might be going on at a deeper level, we can take action from a place of greater awareness. The ability to work with our vulnerability, therefore, provides us with a certain power—to move beyond passive withdrawal and toward relevant action. When individual members possess this kind of skill, it is of great service to the work of the group.

Reflection

WORKING WITH VULNERABILITY IN GROUPS

Consider a specific situation in which you feel vulnerable as a member of a particular group. If a current situation does not come to mind, apply the questions to an experience you've had recently. Once you've identified a situation, take a moment to imagine yourself in the midst of it—the body language and expressions on the faces of others, as well as the tension in your own body and any emotions you feel. When you are ready, move through these questions at a gentle pace.

- IN THE situation you've identified, what is the risk you sense, or what fears do you have?
- WHAT IF that fear or risk happened? What would that mean, in terms of how it might affect you or others, or in terms of how others perceive you?

- HOW MIGHT others be vulnerable?
- WHAT SEEMS to be at stake for the group? Could deadlines be missed, or could conflict cripple the group?
- TAKE A step back, now, for a larger view that includes your personal sense of risk as well as the risk to the group. Do other insights emerge?
- IN THIS situation, how might vulnerability be a teacher for you?
- RECOGNIZING THAT you have choice about bringing more of yourself to the fore or holding back, what actions might you take, to bring your learning to bear on the progress of the group?

Ironically, attending to our vulnerability frees us from being held captive by it. We learn to tap into our emotions as a signal function. Is something afoot? Is someone being made into a scapegoat? Are there inclusion or exclusion issues that need to be addressed? Thus we learn to discern our way through a situation, sensing into the issues and knowing when it's safe to take a stance.

It's no wonder that we feel vulnerable, with our dual need to belong and to be separate. In groups, we express our longing to be seen—to be known for our competence, our intelligence, or the depth of our caring. But the trials of rejection, humiliation, and betrayal give us cause to be defensive. To come to groups as an innocent is to be constantly vulnerable to the unseen and dark aspects of human encounter; yet to be so armored against the sting and lash is to leave no room for learning. We choose to bring ourselves fully, therefore, with our eyes open and a willingness to be vulnerable. And we learn to be discerning about our vulnerability, as we deepen our understanding of groups and ourselves as participants.

11

The Threads of Connection

It is amazing how time and again, one of the most consoling factors in experience is that each experience has a sure structure; this is never obvious to us while we are going through something. But when we look back, we will be able to pick out the path that offered itself. Experience always knows its way. And we can afford to trust our souls much more than we realize. The soul is always wiser than the mind, even though we are dependent on the mind to read the soul for us.[1]

—JOHN O'DONOHUE

Love . . . bears all things, believes all things, hopes all things, endures all things. . . . Love never fails.

—I CORINTHIANS 13

OUR EXPLORATION OF SOUL began through the window of reflection on experience—*of our own experience*. There, we began the journey of ownership, opening to what our experience has taught us, appreciating how it has shaped us, and folding it into our life story.

"Experience always knows its way," O'Donohue writes. Much of this book has been about learning to trust our own experience—learning to see beyond the rational and concrete, and using the mind and physical images to translate for us what our souls already know.

The journey of soul takes us beyond our own internal experience, however, into the realm of action and participation with others. If we don't attend to matters in the world, we'll be lost in the labyrinth of our own soul, where a certain kind of analysis becomes empty and fruitless. Reflection, if it doesn't lead back to actions, becomes merely self-referential, self-absorbed. We may, as O'Donohue suggests, look back upon experience and see the path that has offered itself. But more than that, we learn to value our experience and use it to discern the path that is in front of us—a path of action and participation, connecting us with the souls of others.

When we talk about matters of the soul, therefore, we're talking about the permeable boundary between the inside and outside worlds. To traverse the boundary and make the links, we must be practiced in holding opposites in tension. Learning to sit with the unresolved, without judgment but with *com-passion,* we "suffer with" the conflicting forces in the hope that something more creative will emerge. Thus bearing all things, believing all things, hoping all things, enduring all things—the practice of holding opposites in tension—opens the gateway to love in our lives and work lives.

Learning to hold things in tension is like building muscle strength. We may exercise a muscle group three times a week, each time working it until it fails. Yet we know it's okay, that there's no damage; on the contrary, the muscle recovers itself and becomes stronger. Learning to hold things in tension is an exercise of our lives: In living fully and risking, we inevitably lose and then recover pieces of ourselves, and we become more who we are. There are no techniques or exercises that can solve the riddle of our lives. But learning to hold things in tension strengthens our capacity to endure our experiences, in such a way that we can hold together more of the pieces of ourselves.

Additionally, as we learn to hold opposites in tension, we come to appreciate different ways of seeing, different ways of interacting, different ways of being. Too often in the workplace, emphasis on new ways of thinking tends to be prescriptive—absent of individual creativity, disconnected from what we know to be real. "Focus on the customer." "Empowerment." "Live the values." These injunctions sound promising, but they're abstractions unless they become integrated with the gritty realities of the work setting. In the final pages of this book, we offer no prescriptions, no formulas, no foolproof techniques. The threads we offer are for your own weaving—the threads of awareness and discernment, of listening deeply, of allowing love. We are confident that, as readers, you will find your way back and forth across the boundary between your inner wilderness and your work lives.

Cultivating Awareness and Discernment

The real voyage of discovery lies not in seeing
new landscapes, but in having new eyes.

—MARCEL PROUST

Often in groups, we operate in a conscious world in which most of us agree to exist, never knowing or seeking that other world that lies in the unconscious elements of individuals and groups. Yet it is this second realm in which much of the unifying rhythms of life lie. For those who seek it out, there can be a painful sense of separation, for parts of the journey must be taken alone. Yet what we find there can be extraordinary, as if veils have been lifted revealing an order and pattern and even beauty that we had not known existed.

Our first experience with finding this other world can be challenging, as if we were being asked to see something that just doesn't seem to be there. This experience was vividly illustrated by Edward T. Hall, an anthropologist and a business consultant on cross-cultural communication. Hall filmed a series of encounters at an Indian market in New Mexico. In one particular scene, he describes an encounter between a Caucasian woman and a Pueblo Indian woman selling her pottery:

> Behind the table sat a woman from Santa Clara Pueblo. Watching the white tourist enter the scene, I had to remind myself that what she was doing might not be her fault. She looked at the Pueblo woman and smiled condescendingly. Before my eyes, on the movie screen, the microdrama began to unfold. Holding herself in, the woman began bending forward from the hips to help bridge the gap made by the table, then her arm rose and slowly straightened at shoulder height. My God! It was like a rapier! The extended finger came to rest only inches from the Indian woman's nose and then it stayed there, suspended in midair. Would it never come down? The mouth moved continuously throughout the transaction. . . . After a while the Indian woman's head slowly rotated away from the offending finger deep inside her personal space and an expression of unmistakable disgust covered her face.[2]

Hall asked himself if the unspoken feelings, body language, and the significance of the extended time the finger was pointed at close range would be obvious to an untrained observer. Could other people see these things? To explore his question, he hired a college student, with no background in anthropology, to examine frame by frame the footage he had shot. The student, of course, wanted to know what she should look for. Hall told her he had no idea what she would see but that he wanted her to keep looking at the film until she saw things that were not obvious at first. His one condition was that she keep looking, no matter how boring the exercise. Two days went by and the student returned perplexed. "Dr. Hall, I don't see anything; just a bunch of white people wandering and talking to those Indians." "You haven't been looking long enough," Hall responded. For three weeks, the student pondered the film with no new insights, when suddenly a breakthrough came. With mounting excitement, she brought Hall into the screening room with the frame frozen on the interaction between the two women. "Look at that woman! She's using her finger like a sword as though she is going to push it right through that Indian woman's face. Just look at that finger— the way she uses it. Did you ever see anything like it? Did you see the way that Indian woman turned her face away as though she had just seen something unpleasant?"[3]

Every day from then on, the student reported more and more nuances of interactions between the two cultures. At first it was difficult for her to accept that what she was seeing had been there all along. She had changed, not the film. Hall repeated the experiment multiple times, and each time, often after irritation, puzzlement, and boredom, the student experienced the veil being lifted. "Did you see that?"

With practice over time, awareness of different patterns helps us to see others and our work in new ways, pointing us toward actions that make a difference. Our contribution is more likely to speak to the relevant issues that our work group is struggling with or that go unseen by others. It's the patterns unchecked that often leave us stuck. When a group is silent, for example, what does it mean? acquiescence? agreement? deep thought? resignation? rage?

When we become aware of a pattern, we need to examine it in relation to the group's attention to its task. That's not a straightforward issue, however, and requires patience and discernment. We have to allow room to think about what moves us toward task and what takes us away, in different contexts. Inquiring about an individual's mood, for example, and taking time for the response, may move a group in three ways: The group may move into a personal discussion and completely away from what needs to be done; the discussion may reveal issues in the group that help move the work forward; or the discussion may be personal and off task, but necessary for going forward. The discovery and surprise go both ways. We may think the group is way off track, only to be surprised with how quickly it recovers and how much it gets done; or the group may seem to be cranking out a lot of work, until we discover later that it was totally off base or that important considerations were ignored.

In discerning a group's patterns, we practice working with the question, "Is this in service of the task? And if not, what might it represent?" And we wait to see what else emerges in our awareness. We look beyond the rational. We learn to see with different eyes. We bring all of our experience—our feelings of vulnerability and our understanding of ourselves and of role and groups and patterns. Discernment brings these different dimensions together, appealing to a knowing that is from a deeper layer down than our analysis—the intuitive. It requires stepping back, taking a softer view, with a somewhat hazy focus, as if our eyes are half-closed and we're resting, settling.

When we practice discernment, we learn to trust our own instincts. We recognize that we have our experience and need to trust that within the experience are certain signals. If I'm feeling anxious, or nervous, or have a headache, these are signals that something is going on. It may be that I haven't eaten, or it may be that I'm disturbed by where the conversation is going. By attending to our experience, we learn to discern when something is amiss. We may not always see accurately, and we may become irritated or puzzled or bored trying. Like the students in Hall's experiment, it is only with time and practice that the veil is lifted. "Did you see that?"

The Language of Connectedness

In the 1960s, political philosopher Arthur Koestler coined the term *holon* to express the idea that everything is both a whole and part of a whole. In the journey of soul, this has a simple but profound significance—that we are connected. Sometimes couples attest to this connection, which is not about merging so much as linking, joining—that the other becomes a part of them, a part of their internal psyche, occupying a space that is essentially present regardless of their partner's physical presence or absence. In the context of romantic love, this notion is appealing. In the context of work life, it is less appealing yet no less true.

Imagine the difference it could make in approaching Tom, an annoying and troubled colleague, if I consider that his wholeness is tied to mine. Not that I should become responsible for his wholeness, but that I might be mindful of it—that my approach toward him would be one of respect for his experience of a situation, of tolerance for the bag that drags behind him, of curiosity about what gold might be hidden, of openness toward the parts of him that are difficult as well as the parts that are likable. If Tom's wholeness is tied to mine, I might try approaching Tom in a way similar to how I've learned to approach my own inner wilderness—with compassion, vulnerability, sensitivity to shadow, and a willingness to own "my own stuff."

Often we think of being authentic as going around telling the truth—"being straight," "telling it like it is." While honesty is not to be dismissed, authenticity includes the darker and more complex aspects of being in relationship. To spout off at Tom "honestly" would likely mean a judgmental, one-sided reaction toward his darker side. Being authentic, however, would suggest an acknowledgment of Tom's shadow side, as well as my own, and a willingness to suspend judgment while I hold in tension my own internal conflict about interacting with Tom. Being authentic with Tom implies a deeper layer of relating—recognizing his uniqueness as a human being, that he is more than just an annoying colleague. He is a sojourner, perhaps at a different place on the path than I, but nevertheless a sojourner who struggles with how to bring himself fully, a sojourner whose soul is connected to mine.

How is it that we connect with others across what often seems a chasm? How might we listen to others, so that even in the act of listening we begin to bridge the gulf that separates us? There is a certain form of listening, which is deeper than ordinary conversation, that allows a hidden wholeness to be revealed. In deep listening, we practice being fully present—two beings united by the thread both are following.

Deep listening is a skill that begins with the practice of personal reflection, in which we explore feelings, associations, and images present within us at any given time. In deep listening, we extend this practice outward toward another. We listen to the other without interruption. No easy task. We only listen, careful to not form a response in our head while the person is still talking. This can leave us feeling vulnerable. We respect the silence after someone finishes speaking, not rushing to fill the empty space. This can create anxiety. Yet, while it may be challenging, a healing process is taking place. How many people today feel that they can finish a thought or reflect out loud without being interrupted or caught in a debate? We have lost the art of thinking together, and wholeness eludes us because when analysis and debate dominate, we are speaking in a language of fragmentation.

Through deep listening, we allow the words of another to echo in our mind. As with the practice of personal reflection, we find ourselves associating to feelings, images, stories. And these then become our response. Deep listening nurtures conversation, as love nurtures a friendship. There is no hurry to get anywhere, because you are already in the presence of the one you wish to be with. When two or more people engage in deep listening, there is no straight path or singular outcome, because whatever bubbles up in consciousness is where you're supposed to go.

Deep listening is not practical in many situations, but it is a discipline that can be cultivated as a practical way to reveal the hidden wholeness that lies between us. There is delight at what springs up from the human well of imagination. Images come in and feelings flow, and that's where the richness is. We sense more than is actually said, and we move beyond reaction to discernment. And we learn that the gift of being heard and truly hearing another can be transformative.

Letting Love Flow Through Us

The word *love* can sound awkward in the business setting, where even the mention of feelings can send eyes rolling. It's one of the great absences in our work lives, that we don't acknowledge our need for love and the possibility it can bring to our work. Perhaps a word like love is just too threatening, getting at issues too close to who we are and how we operate. Perhaps all defenses would be down, all vulnerabilities exposed. In this book, however, readers have been invited into a personal journey, a journey that requires both vulnerability and discernment about lowering our defenses—a journey for which love just might have some relevance.

Similar to how we view words like *soul* and *shadow,* as authors we suggest that the mystery surrounding the word *love* is useful. The difficulty in defining the word enables each person to project into it a meaning appropriate to his or her own experience. We invite you, as readers, to draw on your own understanding of love to bring life to these final thoughts. What would it mean to you, if love were allowed to flow through you and into your work setting?

Love expands our capacity. It connects us with what is good and meaningful about our work, fueling our values and passions with energy. It frees us to bring more of our inner truth to bear on what we do, allows us to have greater compassion toward others, and gives us strength to hold in tension the contradictions inherent in the workplace. By creating space for love, we develop appreciation for the path that has led us to where we are, as well as patience to discern the path ahead. We learn new ways of giving that serve others as well as ourselves. It is love that allows us to set aside our personal reactions and open to questions of contribution: *What is the need here? What is possible? What qualities of leadership does this group value? How can I show support for others and give them the space they need to be effective? What tends to move this group forward, and what can I do in service of that?* These questions connect us with the transcendent. And to take up such questions is to invite love to flow through us and into our work.

We cannot escape the wear and tear of work life. Enduring loss and betrayal, as well as love, we are weathered by these experiences and by how we hold them. If we can honor our experience for what it is and see how it has brought us to where we are, we can begin to see the difficulties of work in a new light. What we have endured is written in our faces, our bodies, our eyes; but what we really do with each experience has to do with how we've grown our soul—how we nurture all that is on the inside, that no one can really see.

The consequence of how we learn to honor our experience, therefore, has everything to do with how we retain dignity, fortitude, and solidity. What we face at work becomes part of how we're weathered and honed, how we're made strong or frail, how we enter the next part of our lives. Still, no matter how we attend to it, all that is on the inside will remain something of a mystery. And still, no matter how we open to it, the world we participate in will remain a greater mystery. Such is the nature of soul.

NOTES

Chapter 1: The Inner Wilderness of Soul

1. Loren Eiseley, *The Immense Journey* (New York: Random House, 1957).
2. Carl Jung, *Psychology and Alchemy* (Princeton, NJ: Princeton University Press, 1953), p. 336.
3. Henry David Thoreau, quoted in Phil Cousineau (ed.), *The Soul of the World* (San Francisco: Harper San Francisco, 1993).
4. John O'Donohue, *Eternal Echoes* (New York: Cliff Street Books, 1999), p. 102.
5. David Brower, quoted in Cousineau, *The Soul of the World*.

Chapter 2: Windows to the Soul

1. Cousineau, *The Soul of the World*.

Chapter 3: Soul As a Chorus of Inner Voices

1. Antoine de Saint-Exupéry, *The Little Prince* (New York: Harcourt Brace, 1943), pp. 67–70.

Chapter 4: Shadows of the Soul

1. Carl Jung, quoted in Jolande Jacobi and R.F.C. Hull (eds.), *C.G. Jung: Psychological Reflections* (Princeton, NJ: Princeton University Press, 1970), p. 220.
2. Robert Bly, "The Long Bag We Drag Behind Us," in Connie Zweig and Jeremiah Abrams (eds.), *Meeting the Shadow* (New York: Penguin Putnam, 1991), pp. 6–7.
3. Robert Johnson, *Owning Your Own Shadow* (San Francisco: Harper San Francisco, 1991).
4. John O'Donohue, *Anam Ċara* (New York: Cliff Street Books/ HarperCollins, 1997), p. 85.
5. O' Donohue, *Anam Ċara*, p. 86.

Chapter 5: Playing with Wild Cards

1. Alan Jones, *Soul Making: The Desert Way of Spirituality* (San Francisco: Harper San Francisco, 1985), p. 131.
2. Carl Jung, quoted in Jolande Jacobi (ed.), *C.G. Jung: Psychological Reflections* (New York: Bollingen Foundation, 1953), p. 202.
3. Elie Wiesel, *Souls on Fire: Portraits and Legends of Hasidic Masters* (New York: Summit Books, 1972), p. 164.

Chapter 6: Shadow Sightings and Everyday Practice

1. R. D. Laing, quoted in Zweig and Abrams, *Meeting the Shadow,* pp. xix.
2. Johnson, *Owning Your Own Shadow,* p. 11.
3. Zweig and Abrams, *Meeting the Shadow*, p. xix.
4. Carl Jung, quoted in Jacobi, *Psychological Reflections,* p. 203.
5. Johnson, *Owning Your Own Shadow,* p. x.

Chapter 7: Finding Purpose in Work

1. Chuang Tzu, quoted in Justine Willis Toms and Michael Toms, *True Work* (New York: Bell Tower, 1998), p. 112.

Chapter 10: The Emotional Tapestry of Group Life

1. Carol J. Loomis, "Lies, Damned Lies, and Managed Earnings," *Fortune* (August 2, 1999), p. 84.

Chapter 11: The Threads of Connection

1. John O'Donohue, *Eternal Echos* (New York: Cliff Street Books/ HarperCollins, 1999), p. 243.
2. Edward T. Hall, *The Dance of Life* (New York: Anchor Books/Doubleday, 1983), p. 157.
3. Hall, *The Dance of Life,* pp. 159–160.

INDEX

ABOUT THE AUTHORS

Cheryl Peppers consults in the areas of leadership development, strategic vision, work design, process analysis, team start-ups, and workforce strategy, including several international assignments and consultation in German. Cheryl's clients have included Fortune 500 clients in the chemicals, finance, energy, aerospace, food and beverage, gaming, and high-tech industries, as well as a number of professional service firms.

Principal of Peppers & Associates since December 1997, Cheryl has previously worked as a senior manager with Andersen Consulting, with DDI as a change management consultant, and as an independent contractor with a number of other consulting firms. Formerly an instructor for UCLA Extension in the Business and Management Division, she is an active member of the A.K. Rice Institute, a nonprofit educational institution for the experiential study of leadership and group dynamics. Cheryl has a Ph.D. in organizational psychology from California School of Professional Psychology, an M.A. in cross-culture studies from Fuller Theological Seminary, and a B.S. in education from the University of Wisconsin-Madison.

Contact information: cheryl@peppersandassociates.com

Alan Briskin is author of *The Stirring of Soul in the Workplace,* winner of the 1997 Body Mind Spirit Award of Excellence. The book has been recognized as one of the first to address the role of the human spirit and soul in reconciling the contradictions and polarities many feel in today's workplace. Highly regarded for his commentary on the changing nature of the workplace and work, his articles and observations appear often in the print media. He has spoken throughout the United States and in South Africa on the subject of soul and work and has been a featured guest on National Public Radio.

Alan consults to individuals and organizations in areas of leadership, work design, and learning. He is on the faculty of Saybrook Graduate School and a member of the Fetzer Institute's network of health care professionals advancing the concepts of relationship-centered care. He has a Ph.D. in organizational psychology from The Wright Institute and is a professional associate of the Grubb Institute in London, England.

Contact information: albriskin@aol.com